Heckled From the *Balcony*

A Story About a Pastor Who Had an Affair and What God Taught Him to Bring Him Out of It

A True Story

Jeremiah Kutz

ISBN 978-1-64515-769-4 (paperback)
ISBN 978-1-64515-770-0 (digital)

Copyright © 2019 by Jeremiah Kutz

All rights reserved. No part of this publication may be reproduced, distributed, or transmitted in any form or by any means, including photocopying, recording, or other electronic or mechanical methods without the prior written permission of the publisher. For permission requests, solicit the publisher via the address below.

Christian Faith Publishing, Inc.
832 Park Avenue
Meadville, PA 16335
www.christianfaithpublishing.com

Unless otherwise identified, Scripture quotations are taken from the The Holy Bible, English Standard Version® (ESV), copyright © 2001 by Crossway, a publishing ministry of Good News Publishers. Used by permission. All rights reserved. Scripture quotations marked NIV are taken from THE HOLY BIBLE, NEW INTERNATIONAL VERSION®, Copyright © 1973, 1978, 1984, 2011 by Biblica,

Inc.™ Used by permission. All rights reserved worldwide. Scripture quotations marked NASB are taken from the NEW AMERICAN STANDARD BIBLE®, Copyright © 1960, 1962, 1963, 1968, 1971, 1972, 1973, 1975, 1977, 1995 by The Lockman Foundation. Used by permission.

Printed in the United States of America

To Jesus, my greatest grace.
Without you, my life would still be in the muck and mire.

To my wife, my greatest celebration.
Without you, I would understand less of God's grace and love.
You are the pure vision of what love and grace could be.

To my kids, my greatest joy.
Without you, this book would have been
completed in half the time.

Contents

Foreword 7
Preface 11
Introduction 13
    Part 1: The Affair 17
    Part 2: Reclaiming the Voice of Holy Spirit 35

Grace 41
    Essence of Grace 41
    The Expected Place 42
    Light Roast and Bright-Green Buses 44
    Very Good 49
    Rest 54
    All for You 55
    The Image of God 58
    The Exodus, His Exodus, and My Exodus 61
    Names 66

Celebration 73
    Essence of Celebration 73
    Expectation 75
    Passover 82
    Blades of Grass 86

Shalom	93
In the Middle Of	96
Deer and Callings	100
Joy	**105**
The Essence of Joy	105
Dance	107
Living Water	113
A Good Bottle of Wine	118
Gratitude	122
Answers or Responses	125
Life	128
Afterword	**131**
The Afterword to the Afterword	137
Notes	**139**

Foreword

I am a pastor, not just any pastor; I was Jeremiah's pastor for the five years that he spent in Pennsylvania. During those years I became his pastor, mentor and friend. The story you are about to read is real. Well, not just real, it's transparent and perhaps not just transparent, but painfully transparent. You see I know the story because I lived it with Jeremiah and Elisha.

I will never forget the phone call that informed me that they were in trouble. Nor will I forget standing in a hotel lobby on the phone with Jeremiah as he tearfully confessed that he had lied to me about the extent of his affair. As a leader in our denomination I had taken his part; I stood up for him, and I did so with the passion of a friend and a mentor. Now I heard him say that he had lied to me, covered his sin, and left me holding the bag. I had a choice. I could be angry or I could be like Jesus.

This book is not just about being like Jesus; it is about finding out what Jesus is really like. Each page drips with personal transparency, internal struggle, the pain and uncertainty that so many pastors deal with in silence, and the real-life struggle to keep a marriage alive. It is the story of how grace wins and a story about the reality of redemption. In a world of brokenness, it speaks of the Jesus who never gives up on us. In a disposable society, it speaks to the power of a wife who will not give up. Elisha has walked the way of suffering bearing the cross of a disciple (Luke 9:23). She bears its scars, but more importantly, she is crowned with its victory. Elisha has demonstrated the glory of God in suffering and in healing.

I chose to be like Jesus in that hotel lobby not because I am perfect or because I have it all together. I did it because I didn't know any other way. You see I love Jeremiah and Elisha. We have walked the road of faith, failure, hope and redemption together. The Apostle Paul, writing to the church in Corinth, says "love is not provoked, does not take into account a wrong suffered, does not rejoice in unrighteousness but rejoices in the truth". (I Cor 13:5b-6) I told Jeremiah that telling the whole truth would lead to the final part of his healing. Perhaps this book serves as a testament to that fact.

For men (especially pastors) who struggle with secrets, who bury the real deep beneath the mask, who struggle with real life pressures, shame, guilt, and temptation, this book is for you. For wives who are tempted to give up, this book is encouragement to fight for the promises of God. For those buried in guilt and shame, whose inner voice heckles them with accusations of unworthiness and self-loathing, this book is a beacon of hope.

Last summer I had the great honor of presiding over a ceremony where Jeremiah and Elisha renewed their marriage vows. During the ceremony we used a Mikvah, as part of the service. The tradition of Mikvah (ceremonial cleansing) dates back to the earliest days of Israel. During that ceremony I used the following words:

> *Jeremiah and Elisha as you enter these waters enter them as a symbol of the Holy Spirits presence. As you immerse yourselves in these waters find in them a symbol of the burial of your old lives, your old marriage, and your old covenants. Find in the washing a ceremonial purification of past failures, past sorrows, and pain. Leave buried in them all that has gone before. Come out of these waters renewed in your walk with Christ, your faith in Him, and your*

faith in each other. Come again to this spot washed clean and prepared to enter into a new marriage covenant before God.

    This is a picture of the redemption you will find in the pages of this book. As you enter the waters of its pages, dear brother or sister, find in them the redemption of Jesus, the hope of grace, the wonder of forgiveness and the love of God.

Dan Cale
Lead Pastor
Hughesville Friends Church

Endorsement

    Jeremiah, along with his wife Elisha, will lead you on a raw vulnerable journey, of what could have been a major defeat in their marriage and walk with God, and give you the hope that Jesus is in the job of restoration, redemption, and intimacy with us. Jeremiah's book will give you hope and a plan for intimacy with Christ.

Dr. Nick Gough, D.min, MTS
Senior Pastor
FaithCenter Church
www.efaithcenter.com

Preface

I had an affair.

I thought that sentence would be a great way to kick this off.

After the affair, my life was full of depression, anxiety, shame, guilt, and fear. Yet Holy Spirit whispered great truths in my ear that allowed to me to rise above the great sadness and walk in his identity: grace, celebration, and joy. This book is about those truths.

This project is what the Father taught me to usher me into my destiny. As you read, you will become aware of many unanswered questions and maybe a lack of explanation for certain ideas. This is intentional. I have purposefully left many of these sections unanswered and open-ended. The idea is that Holy Spirit would speak to you the answers that would affect you personally.

My goal is that you would walk away with questions that would drive you to the depth of Scripture and to the heart of Jesus. This is coming from one who desires truth over tradition. I love learning from the past; I value the sacrifices from generations who have gone before me. But tradition never trumps truth.

The Bible says we are a new creation with a new song singing a new purpose. There's something new about that. So maybe Holy Spirit desires to teach you something new. And it's all about Jesus, and that's truth. He will heal you.

If you are struggling with depression, anxiety, oppression, fear, uncertainty, or [insert your struggle here], then my prayer is that you understand the grace, celebration, and joy that only Jesus can give. This book is for those who struggle with something. Whatever it is for you, it's not the end. It can be healed, restored, and reset. You can learn to use it for the glory of God.

My prayer is that these truths that ushered me into a new creation will do the same for you. Know that you are covered in prayer even as you read this book. May Holy Spirit guide you and comfort you as you set off on this adventure. May a new song emerge in your heart, and may you sing it loudly.

Introduction

I wanted the title of this book to be *My Inner Voice Was a Jackass (King James Version)*. However, wanting to appeal to a broad range of moral, ethical, and spiritual audiences, I chose otherwise. But that doesn't make it any less true.

See, I have this inner voice. Not voices in my head, but this inner monologue (or narration, if you will) that wakes me up in the morning and suggests certain decisions throughout the day. More importantly, this voice tells me what I should believe about my standing, my purpose, and my identity. And I'm guessing that you do as well, even if you don't recognize it.

But mine was a little rascal. Remember the two old guys from *The Muppets*, Waldorf and Statler? They would sit safely in their upper balcony and yell out, heckle, accuse, and jeer at those on stage. Their sarcasm was hilarious—if you weren't the one on stage. I loved those guys; they were the only reason I watched *The Muppets*. Well… them and the Swedish chef.

Yet that was my daily inner narration. I would wake up before my alarm to the jeers: "You suck!" "You're not good enough!" "You're not smart enough!" "God can't use you. You've messed up!" "You've made a lot of mistakes. Today will be another!" "Well, Jeremiah is really taking a beating on this show. It's hard to feel bad for him. We take a beating every show."

At first, I shrugged it off. I knew who I was, and I am good enough; I'm smart enough; and doggone it, people like me—after all, I was a pastor for almost twelve years with churches that loved and encouraged me. I gave countless sermons and teachings on having confidence and boldness, that we are created with divine identity. And a couple of them were good. I knew what to believe; I knew the right things to say; I knew the powerful things to pray.

Yet those hecklers continued their taunt; and after a while, I began to try and prove them wrong. Rather than believing the truth of my divine identity,[1] I settled into the ocean of self-doubt, restlessness, and a work-based religion. I began to believe that I must prove Waldorf and Statler wrong.

Rather than searching out the deep things of God, rather than pursuing the power of Holy Spirit, rather than taking risk in bringing the kingdom of God here to earth, I began proving that I was smart enough, that I was good enough, strong enough, handsome enough, and perfect enough. The pursuit of God evolved into the pursuit of perfection—the perfect me. When focus, attention, and intent rest on self, the only natural expression is arrogance, selfishness, and entitlement.

It's the McDonald's philosophy in motion: I deserve a break today. I deserve a better job. I'm working hard; I deserve a better truck. My wife or husband doesn't make me feel good; I deserve a different spouse. My name isn't famous; I deserve a different life. [Insert your thoughts here.] This is the only expectant outcome of pride and arrogance. What's in it for me? How does this affect me? How does this decision make me feel good? How does this decision prove that I'm smart enough, good enough, handsome enough? How does this choice prove that I deserve something better? When in reality, we deserve nothing. It is only out of grace that we receive anything.

So here lies the great paradox: Why does the weaker voice of self shout louder than the strongest voice that created the universe? And why do I deeply believe the jeers of Waldorf and Statler more so than the loving-kindness of Papa God?

How does that happen? If truth were told, I would wager that a majority of you reading this struggle with this as well to some extent. Perhaps the hecklers are quieter, less sarcastic, or less frequent. Maybe for some, they are significantly louder. Maybe for some of you, they have become so common, you forget that they're there; you have already settled into believing them, and they have become a way of life. Wherever you are, there is another way.

Let me explain it this way. In the beginning of time, God created a garden. In this garden, he planted two trees: the tree of life and the tree of knowledge of good and evil. To Adam and Eve, he explained that they could eat from any tree, just not from the one he planted directly in the center of the garden, just not from the one that the eyes take delight in the most, just don't eat from that tree. You know, the one that I made most appealing to you…

Yeah, just don't eat from that one.

Uh…okay.

Why the other tree? Woven into the eternal fabric of a life of grace, celebration, and joy is this concept of free will. At the essence of humanity is choice. You must have a choice. In order to experience grace in its truest form, you must be able to choose selfishness. To experience celebration in its divine nature, you must have an option to choose entitlement. If divine joy is to be experienced in your life, the choice for hate must exist.

If the goodness of God were the only thing available, the only thing to ever be experienced, how would you know that it was even good in the first place? If there were no other option except the loving-kindness of God, how would you know it is loving-kindness?

There must be another tree. And with every decision you face, a second tree is planted. Two trees; two voices; one choice.

The tree of life, or perhaps the voice of life, beckons its hearer to believe the truth of *imago Dei*, that we were created in the image of God with divine purpose and intent. Our identity rests with the truth that we are already loved and accepted by Papa God just as we are, right now.

Out of the tree of the knowledge of good and evil, the voice of pride, arrogance, and entitlement speaks. This tree challenges the very words of God, twisting them into some deformed train wreck where you just can't take your eyes off it.

Oh how my inner voice loved that tree. So much so that I chose to have an affair. I chose the fruit of selfishness, arrogance, pride, and entitlement. I chose the voice of ego and self. I believed that tree. That's what this book is about: how I house-trained my inner voice that heckled me from the balcony and replaced it with another voice, a voice of grace, joy, and celebration—the identity and voice of Holy Spirit—and how you can too.

Part 1

The Affair

The Biggest Mistake of My Life

I was going to write out the story of what happened with all the juicy details because, after all, that kind of stuff sells books, right? Halfway through, I realized that this is not what I want this book to be about. So I highlighted it and pushed delete.

Instead, what you will read in the few pages below is the testimony that my wife and I have given in various group settings.

> Because I want you to hear her heart
> her heart that hurt
> yet her heart of forgiveness
> of pursuit
> of strength
> and of grace

I want you to hear how my reckless inner voice finally bested me, how I relented and chose the "other" tree, yet how God rescued me, and how I finally found the essence of grace through a God who pursued me and a wife who loved me unconditionally.

So without further ado, I give you the "Essence of Grace."

* * * * *

JEREMIAH. Hey, everybody. I'm Jeremiah, and this is my super foxy bride of seventeen years, Elisha. We want to tell you our story of hurt and brokenness and how God pursued us with grace and forgiveness.

Our story begins in 1998. I was finally coming back to God after several years of the party scene in college. I had allowed friends to persuade me to party with them, and party I did.

But that is always the empty life. Nothing good ever comes from that kind of life.

So I woke up one day and decided that was enough. I had felt hollow and numb for so long, but I knew the way of Jesus. I had grown up in a Christian home with parents who loved God. They took me to church every Sunday, and I learned to appreciate and respect that way of life. I could tell you what my parents believed, but I didn't know who God was to me.

In high school, I started attending youth group and had an unbelievable youth pastor. He is one of the greatest disciplers of this generation, and he invested a ton of time into me. I had attended over twenty-five mission trips in my four years in high school. I loved and respected my youth pastor. I could tell you what he believed, but I didn't know who God was to me.

So when I attended Malone College in 1993, jumping into the wrong crowd was easy. I had a ton of friends, and we partied all the time. But now, in early 1998, as I sat there in bed after that night of partying, I had enough.

See, Jesus was pursuing me all along, but I was numb to his voice. But now, that fire in my heart was reignited. I got in contact with my youth pastor again, and I reconnected with God. I had fallen in love with him and finally began to know who he was to me.

So what do you do when you become a passionate follower of God again? That's right, you get a Christian girlfriend—that's just what you do. So I was dating a nice Christian girl for several months as I was learning who I was all over again. But one night, it all changed.

My youth-pastor friend invited me to a church party. He said there was someone there he wanted me to meet. I walked in, and he introduced me to this angel leaning against the wall. Oh, good Lord, she was gorgeous. So we talked for a bit; and immediately, I was attracted to her.

But there was a hitch. she was only seventeen. I was so mad at my youth-pastor friend; I thought he was nuts. So I walked out of that church disappointed but ready to wait until she was a bit older. And that nice Christian girl I had been dating? Yep, I broke up with her that week. So after Elisha's eighteenth birthday, I went to work to win this angel's heart.

Elisha. I was raised in a Christian home with parents who loved God. They raised me to be independent and strong, so staying away from the wrong crowd was easy. I was going God's way, and no one was going to stop me.

Throughout high school, I was a good girl, never getting into too much trouble, just sometimes dating the wrong guys. I was heavily involved in church and saturated my life with Jesus.

When I was a sophomore in high school, we got a new youth pastor, the same guy whom Jeremiah had as his youth pastor. He was awesome and changed my life forever. He discipled me, mentored me, and taught me how to be a genuine Christian.

Now I had graduated high school at seventeen, ready to get on with what God had for me. And one day at a church party, my youth pastor introduced me to a handsome twenty-two-year-old. He was hot, and we hit it off. But when I told him I was seventeen, he immediately backed off. I was disappointed, but I understood. We didn't talk again for almost a year.

One day, I was hanging out with my youth pastor and some other friends. He was trying to set me up with another guy. Jeremiah stopped in to say hi to my youth pastor. I couldn't take my eyes off him. After he left, I turned to my youth pastor and said, "Hook me up with that one."

Shortly after I turned eighteen, Jeremiah became a youth pastor intern at my church, and we were back in business. We started dating immediately and spent a ton of time with each other. We loved each other with, as tacky as it sounds, an endless love. I never doubted even once that Jeremiah loved me with all his heart even more than he loved himself.

So a year and a half later, when he bent down on one knee and asked me to marry him, it was an easy and excited yes! I couldn't wait to spend the rest of my life with him. I was so excited to be called Mrs. Kutz, or Cutz, or Klutz, or Kurtz, or just Jeremiah's wife.

JEREMIAH. On June 24, 2000, I watched this angel walk down the aisle and place her tiny hand in mine. I couldn't believe such a beautiful woman could possibly love a skinny big-eared kid. But she did. I was the luckiest guy on the face of the planet.

God had miraculously called me to be a pastor, that story another time, and we were anxious to get started extending the kingdom of God everywhere. It was Elisha and I against the world!

ELISHA. I married Jeremiah when I was nineteen years old. We were so in love and ready to conquer the world for Jesus. When we had been married a year, we left for the mission field. We served two years with the Navajo Indian tribe.

After our term was up, we headed to a church in Pennsylvania where Jeremiah took a youth-pastor / associate-pastor position for five years. During those years, we had our two girls, Makiah and Eden.

Parenthood wasn't what I expected. Both girls did not sleep, and Makiah cried for the first year, it seemed, non-stop. It was a very rough start to motherhood. I felt that the girls constantly needed my attention from every bit of me. I felt that Jeremiah understood and could take care of himself. And I began pushing his needs aside.

I thought it was just a phase or stage of life, and that everything would eventually get better, that one day they would sleep through the night, and I wouldn't feel so miserable. And Jeremiah understood all this, right?

JEREMIAH. No, he didn't. The two girls always had her attention, and it felt as if I was a second, sometimes a third thought in her life. I loved my two girls, but I felt as if I were trying to compete for Elisha's attention. Although I never resented the girls, I had begun to resent Elisha.

I know the logical question you all are thinking. "At what point did you communicate that feeling to your wife?" Great question! I'm glad you asked it. See, I was never good at communication. It was modeled for me to just squish everything to the inside. So rather than having a healthy conversation with my wife about what I was feeling, I stuffed it all down deep and allowed it to fester and grow. Although very small, a wall had begun to be built between us. Neither one of us recognized it just yet, but it was there.

In 2007, I began experiencing a restlessness in my life. I began to dive into a new essence of theology, and it shook me to the core. I began reading as much as I could about it and couldn't get enough. When you're confronted with a new reality that shakes the very core of your existence, you have two options. First, fall to God and search for truth with everything you have. Or two, fall away; give in to doubt, chaos, and confusion; and let that have its way. I chose number two.

Listen, your relationship with your spouse is a direct reflection of your relationship with Jesus, and my relationship with Jesus was simply business casual. The only time I ever opened the Bible was to prepare teachings. My prayer life was nonexistent, and I began to have real doubts that God was even real to begin with.

ELISHA. Toward the end of the five years, I could see that Jeremiah was sensing a restlessness. We had talked about it and thought that maybe God was calling him out of youth ministry and into something else, but we weren't sure what.

So he took the position of Young Adult Pastor at a church in Ohio and also the Youth Ministry Specialist position for the denominational headquarters. I could see that Jeremiah was becoming more and more restless.

I could see his personality change. He was making comments and acting out in ways that were not the man I married. He was becoming someone different. He started to get more and more depressed, and I didn't know what to do.

I thought it would eventually go away, and it was just a season in our marriage, maybe even a midlife crisis. He said he was getting old and didn't do anything meaningful for God. After all, he was thirty-five, you know.

JEREMIAH. I remember teaching on a Sunday morning. I paused midway through the sermon. To me, it felt like twenty minutes. To everyone else seated there, it seemed as if I lost my place for a few seconds. But I paused and had this intense conversation with myself. "Is this even true? I'm not sure I even believe what I'm teaching? What am I doing up here? God, are you even real?"

I didn't enjoy my job. I wasn't enjoying my marriage. I wasn't enjoying life. Depression had sunk in. I remember thinking, "What next?"

ELISHA. April 2010, I got pregnant with our son Judah. By now, our girls were awesome, great sleepers and total daddy's girls. But Jeremiah thought we were done, and he was happy with his two girls.

And surprise! We were pregnant. I guess you could say it was the straw that broke the camel's back. Jeremiah completely withdrew from me. I didn't know who he was because he was not acting as himself.

I remember diving into the Word and praying so much for him. Months had gone by. He had been gone a lot, traveling with his Youth Specialty position, and I was lonely at times.

JEREMIAH. I never let anyone know where I was in life. I pretended that all was good. I lied constantly about what I was thinking and feeling to everyone, including my wife. And then surprise…another baby? Are you kidding me? I don't know why I was surprised, I know how those things happen.

But when Elisha showed me that white stick with the two blue lines on it, I didn't say a word and walked out of the room, jumped in my truck, and drove off crying.

It was the perfect storm. I hated my job, I hated life, no relationship with Jesus, and a dying relationship with my wife. I began hanging out with a young woman from a small group I was leading who, at the time, I believed made me feel good about life. We would text and call and see each other often. Rather than spending time with God and my wife, I would spend time with her.

ELISHA. In 2010, when I was six months pregnant, Jeremiah called me and said he was coming home early from his trip. He said he had something to tell me, and it couldn't wait.

Little did I know that my world was about to fall apart. He said he had something to confess to me. He told me he was having an affair. I was absolutely dumbfounded and completely heartbroken.

Yet this fight welled up inside of me. A fight I never knew existed. I remembered speaking out loud, "Satan had the power, but he was not going to have it anymore."

JEREMIAH. I told her I was having an affair, subconsciously wanting and expecting her to kick me to the curb. But to my surprise, she fought, and she fought hard. Yet I wasn't ready, nor did I want to come back.

My shame, guilt, depression, and selfishness took precedence in every decision I made. It was all about me, why couldn't anyone see that?

ELISHA. The next six months were absolutely brutal. I cried every single day for six months. I had no idea I could even cry that many tears. I remember picking up toys with my girls, and I just started to weep. One of them asked me if I was okay and then said, Mommy, you should call daddy because he will make you feel better.

Little did they know what I really wanted to do to their daddy.

JEREMIAH. I cried every single day for six months, not because someone hurt me, but because I had deemed myself worthless, insignificant, and useless. The affair had ended, but I had given up my identity, given up my calling, and given up my joy.

The guilt and shame had become mountains of emotion every single day. I would wake up to the voices of worthlessness and at night drift off to sleep with the weight of guilt on me.

The hopelessness and depression were so unbearable. I remember one day being completely under the weight of this hopelessness and depression. I took my pistol out, pulled the bolt back, and put it to my head, and then in my mouth, crying and shaking, just wanting to feel peace again.

It was like the weight of the world was on me, pressing down harder and harder. I couldn't breathe. So when I took my pistol out, it was out of desperation…until I heard my girls laugh downstairs.

Jesus is grace.

Elisha. I never lost my desire to fight. I fought for him to stay, to love me again, to feel forgiven, to feel grace. During these months, I felt God's fight inside of me every single day. He was my only hope, my only chance to bring Jeremiah back to us.

"But one thing I do. forgetting what lies behind and straining forward to what lies ahead, I press on toward the goal for the prize of the upward call of God in Christ Jesus" (Philippians 3:13).

I believed that God would bring beauty from these ashes. I not only believed it, but I claimed it. It was mine for the taking, and I was taking hold of it. We were going to endure and come out victorious.

I surrounded myself with godly women who believed in both of us, who were our biggest cheerleaders and would not let us fail. I bathed in the Word of God and taped scripture all over the house and in my car.

I saturated my life with Jesus and inhaled his life every chance I got. He endured for me, my friends endured for me, because I would never have been able to do it alone.

JEREMIAH. It was February of 2011. Although I was no longer a pastor, I forgot to give my church keys back to the church. The hopelessness and depression had taken their toll. I was done. The only thing left to do was to fall to God. So I took the keys and let myself into the church. I went to the altar.

I wish I could say that I saw the heavens open, Jesus descend, and doves fly through the sanctuary, but they didn't. There was no voice, no singing, no lights. All I did was fall to my knees and say, "No more, God. I'm done." My stake had been driven into the ground, and I was not returning.

ELISHA. You see, from the very beginning of the confession, Jeremiah was constantly telling me how sorry he was for what he had done, but I felt like it was just words to make himself feel better. I knew that one day he would come to me and be broken and truly sorry.

That night, when he came back from the church, he hugged me and just wept uncontrollably. It seemed like for hours. He asked for forgiveness, and that's when I knew he was truly sorry and was ready to move forward in our relationship.

Right now, he has the most precious relationship with Jesus, and this time it is not because he is getting paid to. I've seen us both go from broken to beautiful. We definitely received our beauty from the ashes.

JEREMIAH. Although I know God has forgiven, that he has cast all my sin as far as the east is from the west, I had wrestled with forgiving myself. There was a daily fight for a true understanding of how God views me. "But you are a chosen race, a royal priesthood, a holy nation, a people for his own possession, that you may proclaim the excellences of him who called you out of darkness into his marvelous light" (1 Peter 2:9).

The most significant words in this verse are "you are." You are…not "you may become one day," or "if only you do this then you will be this," but rather, you are. Now, as I sit here today, just as I am and just as you are, God sees us as these things. And if we could live under this truth on a daily basis, how much could we do with the kingdom of God?

A key verse for me was 1 Corinthians 3:21–22: "For all things are yours, whether Paul or Apollos or Cephas or the world or life or death or the present or the future—all are yours." What is obviously missing from the list? The past.

The present and the future are ours, but not the past. Why? Why isn't the past ours? Because it was bought and paid for by the blood of Jesus. The past is not ours. It's his. And there is no condemnation for those in Christ.

And when I actually began to believe that, forgiving myself was easy.

ELISHA. Today, our marriage is more than I could have ever imagined. I am still in awe of how God can take something so painful and make it into something so beautiful. Every day I get to wake up and thank God for his restoration power and how he can take two sinful people and make them powerful together despite what Satan tried to destroy.

I have learned that communication is one of the most important things we can do for our marriage. That men and women are so different and not to assume that the other person knows what you are thinking. Always be vulnerable enough to share what is on your mind.

I've learned that forgiveness is hard but completely necessary if you want to move on and heal. Because honestly, it's too hard not to forgive. There are way too many things you have to keep dealing with if you don't learn to forgive.

"Bear with each other and forgive one another if any of you has a grievance against someone. Forgive as the Lord forgave you" (Colossians 3:13).

And the most important thing that I've learned is that God has to be the center of your marriage. Not just say he is but make him the center of your marriage. You must pray together, read his word together, and grow in him together. Your marriage should reflect your relationship with Christ.

JEREMIAH. Today, our marriage is unbelievably satisfying. God has redeemed and fully restored my relationship with Elisha even beyond my wildest dreams. Although I still have much to learn, I am pursuing her with passion. God has taken the broken pieces of a selfish and shattered life and a broken marriage, and through his grace and love, put everything back together even stronger than it was before.

Although I have not perfected the art of communication, I am getting better at it, right, Sweetie? And I can honestly say that I love her more than I love myself.

Both of us understand that our marriage would never be the same again. And in order for it to become powerful, one would have to choose forgiveness and the other choose redemption. It would only become what we made it.

We believed, and so we did. And you can too.

Elisha. We want to leave you with four ways to put a hedge around your marriage. Although these are not all the actions you can do, these are four from our story. Because we not only want to tell you our story, but we want you to protect yours.

"Finally be strong in the Lord and in the strength of his might. Put on the whole armor of God, that you may be able to stand against the schemes of the devil" (Ephesians 6:10–11).

1. Be aware of the little things that can lead to something bigger and then deal with them so they don't later become a perfect storm.

2. Surround yourself with godly friends who will fight for you, not against you.
3. Pray with each other and for each other. Read the Word of God together. That's what strengthens the bonds of love.
4. Offer grace constantly because Grace + Truth + Time = Forgiveness.

We celebrated seventeen years of marriage last year by renewing our vows together with new promises. We celebrated what the Lord has done and is doing in our lives.

We choose to share our testimony with others to encourage and show the healing power of God that is offered to every marriage, not just ours.

"Oh give thanks to the Lord for he is good, his steadfast love endures forever. Let the redeemed of the Lord say so, whom he has redeemed from trouble" (Psalm 107:1–2).

We want to proclaim that marriages can be healed, can be amazing, and to never go down without a fight because some things are just worth fighting for.

* * * * *

She is amazing, isn't she? And thank you, Jesus, for your pursuit.

Part 2

Reclaiming the Voice of Holy Spirit

Words

Communication is the heartbeat of civilization. In every culture, in every era, people find ways to effectively communicate with each other. Humanity was created with a sense of community and connection. We must find ways to share feelings, ideas, loves, and hates. We are always finding new ways to express ourselves: art, stories, movies, drama, Facebook, Instagram, and Snapchat.

Humanity was created for community, dialogue, and communication. It's interesting, if you are in prison and disobey the prison laws, sometimes you have food taken away; sometimes you are beaten, whipped, or crucified. Yet those seldom work. So the prison authority found a more effective punishment. If you disobey prison laws, you are simply placed in what they call solitary confinement.

Solitary confinement. Locked in a cell with no interaction with any other human being. That's the punishment. No communication with humanity. No ways to share feelings, ideas, loves, and hates. No dialogue with anyone. And it works. Even the hardest criminals obey the prison laws to avoid that kind of hell. We were created for communication and community.

Humanity will always find a way to communicate. In order to do that, we use sounds, which we call words. Words make an attempt for someone to express their ideas and feelings in picture form, without actually creating a tangible picture. This picture allows one to connect to and be drawn toward another. In other words, when someone feels a connection with another person, they can see, understand, and value the picture that has been communicated.

Some are better than others at painting the picture. My wife is excellent at communication. She can hold down a conversation with anyone. Everyone who meets her and talks with her for just a few minutes will walk away saying, "Wow, I felt like the only one in the entire room. She's now my best friend."

I, on the other hand, suck at it. People often look for a way out. Now my wife does give me props; she often says how much better I'm getting at it. Although I do feel like a child sometimes when she says, "Jeremiah, use your words." Uh…fine.

Humanity was destined to communicate. Yet in our abstract English language, it is often difficult to see the picture being painted. But not in Hebrew, the language of the Old Testament and the words of Jesus. Hebrew is a very picture-oriented language. In fact, if you miss the picture, you miss the deep, profound, divine meaning.

Now, Hebrew is a poor language. By poor I mean the vocabulary is minimal. There are only 8,679 unique words in the Hebrew Old Testament. That may seem like a bunch of words. However, by comparison, the English language has 171,476 unique words, with more nonsensical words being added every day like *bootylicious, humblebrag, mumblecore, anyhoo,* and *yowza.*

Anyhoo, those 8,679 unique words compose the total word count of the Hebrew Old Testament at 419,687. In other words, there are only 8,679 words in the biblical Hebrew vocabulary and that small vocabulary makes up the 419,687 total words in the Old Testament. With those minimal unique words comprising that large a word count, words must mean many different things. Thus, the Hebrew language becomes richer, deeper, and fuller as the words paint a picture that engages, challenges, and enriches the essence of the soul.

Let me give you an example. The Hebrew word for "corner" is *kanaph*. We read about this in Numbers 15:38, "Speak to the people of Israel, and tell them to make tassels on the corners of their garments throughout their generations, and to put a cord of blue on the tassel of each corner." This is the beginning of the Jewish prayer shawl. This tradition still continues today. In fact, Jesus, a Jewish rabbi, would have worn this in keeping with the law.

Now what's fascinating is that the word *kanaph* also means "wing." A bird has one *kanaph* or two *kanaphim*. We see this word used in Malachi 4:2, "The sun of righteousness will rise with healing in its wings."

Or we could translate this phrase in Malachi as "the sun of righteousness will rise with healing in its corners." Corners of what? The prayer shawl. Someone is coming who will heal through the corners. In Luke 8, a woman was suffering from an illness and couldn't find help. She meets Jesus and reaches out for his *kanaph*, and she was healed. She believed Malachi 4, that Jesus was the "sun of righteousness" with healing in his wings/corners.

Unless you understand the depth of the Hebrew language, you may miss out on the richness that is available. This is where reclamation of the inner voice begins. Not with the Hebrew language, but with the awareness that God is communicating with us in profound ways, with brush strokes that paint the vitality of his goodness.

The Here and Now

There's an ancient story in Genesis 28 where a man named Jacob spends the night in a place called Bethel. He fell asleep and had a great dream of angels ascending and descending a ladder. God speaks and gives him some amazing promises for his life. Jacob wakes up and says, "Surely the Lord is in this place and I did not know it."[2] Jacob is waking up to God, who is always here regardless of situations, experiences, feelings, and circumstances. He is a God of "here and now."

The start of knowing about God is simply paying attention, being fully present where you are right here, right now.[3] But some of us are going so fast, we miss out on the holiness and significance of God. Maybe the thing we are wrestling most, within this culture, is realizing that the ground we are standing on is holy.

I went on a trip with my grandpa and grandma when I was in junior high. We drove to Fort Sill, Oklahoma, to see their daughter (my aunt) and her husband who was stationed there. Now, I have an enjoyable setback whenever I travel. If I am not driving, I could sleep within the first five to ten minutes of a trip and sleep nearly the whole time. If my wife is driving, I could fall asleep before we get to Walmart.

So I slept much of the way to Oklahoma, and my grandpa would get so frustrated. He would wake me up and say, "Jeremy, see that tree? You'll never see that tree again." I would roll my eyes and go back to sleep. But what was my grandpa doing? He was waking me up to see the here and now.

How many times have you and I been so caught up in the moment of life that we miss what God has for us? How many of us are wrestling with busyness and are so preoccupied with going and going and going that we miss the significance of God in everything around us?

What have we missed? You know there won't be any tears in heaven, but I bet that might take a while. When we get there and look back on what we missed in everyday life—how we were so busy running and running—and we look back and see what God had for us, and we missed it...I don't know. I think we'll shed some tears.

God wants to know you and pull you into his divine purposes, but we are moving so fast, and we are listening to so many other voices, and we're talking with this person, and we're dealing with that addiction and insecurity, and we're going and going and going from this meeting to this class to this job to this event. Is it possible for even Christians to go from one Christian thing to another Christian thing so fast that they miss the significance of who God is even in the ordinary?

God is right here, right now—his very presence available at any time, in any place, speaking to you. Stop. Breathe. Don't just breathe, but feel the air move…past your tongue, causing it to chill just slightly. Feel your lungs move in and out as you hear your own breath leave your body and then return.

Take a moment to hear the small click when you close your mouth and your teeth come together. Inhale deeply and smell the aroma of life as it passes in front of you. It marches on right in front of us regardless of whether or not we pay attention.

And then close your eyes and listen. If you listen long enough, you can feel the faint rhythm of your heart beating just inside your chest. It's here, in that red beating muscle, the God of here and now speaks. And we must wake up to this reality. We must tune into his frequency. We must realize the divine implications of hearing the divine voice as it thunders or whispers across our hearts.

Grace

"The realization that no matter where you are,
you are in the presence of the Lord."

—Ann Spangler

Essence of Grace

The idea of grace in the Jewish world is a curious topic. In English, we can formulate an expression or ideal of what we believe to be the essence of grace, so we come up with a definition…because in the Western world, that's just what we do. Everything needs a definition. Thus, we say the definition of grace is "unmerited favor." Or grace means grace and that's just what grace means. Yet in the Hebrew language, it is impossible to define grace. The Jewish people couldn't imagine reducing the divine qualities of God to a mere definition.

See, grace isn't defined; it is experienced. You can't tell me what grace is; you must show me. Grace was meant to arrive into one's life like the warmth of a fire. The only way we could possibly understand fire is through its expression.

I could give an Eskimo a logical definition of fire: the combustion or burning, in which substances combine chemically with oxygen from the air and typically give out bright light, heat, and smoke. In addition, the English had two roots for fire: *paewr* and *egni* (source of Latin *ignis*). The former was "inanimate," referring to fire as a substance; and the latter was "animate," referring to it as a living force. Make sense, Mr. Eskimo?

He's a polite Eskimo, so he would thank me yet continue to shiver. He would even say that he understands fire and appreciates the in-depth commentary that led to his vital comprehension of the essence of fire, yet he would continue to shiver. He may even run to his village and tell his family and friends about the beauty of fire, yet they would all continue to shiver. He may even invite those same people to the front of his house to, let's say an altar, to accept the truth that fire is warm, and all of them would agree, "Yes, we believe that fire is warm." Yet they would continue to shiver.

They would then commission other Eskimos to travel to remote areas throughout Siberia and Greenland expressing the ideals of fire and warmth. "Just believe," they would say, yet all of them would continue to shiver.

You get my point? It isn't until I light the match and create a fire that the true understanding of fire emerges. Likewise, grace must be experienced, not simply defined. And boy, did I ever experience it.

After my affair, God's grace left me wide-eyed, with my mouth dropped open, in awe of the fire. And I soaked in every waft of its warmth. Every molecule of its heat I absorbed. I let none past. It started when I heard God whisper, "Where are you?"

The Expected Place

There's a story in Genesis 3 where God asked Adam and Eve the peculiar question: "Where are you?" It's only peculiar because he's God and already knew the answer to the question in the first place. Yet he asked it anyways.

HECKLED FROM THE BALCONY

The Hebrew language has two words for where. The first is *ephoh*, which asks a question about geographical location: Where is Starbucks? Where in the world did those Eskimos go?

The second use of where does not mean a location. The word, *'ayyeh* expresses a surprise, not of the unexpected, but rather a proclamation that something wasn't where it was expected. God asked Adam, "Where are you?" not to find him; instead, to express that he was not in the expected place...by his side. "Where are you? You're supposed to be here with me." But Adam hid.

The affair had ended, but I was hiding from others, from God, from myself. I was packed full of shame, guilt, worthlessness, and embarrassment. I couldn't look a majority of people in the eyes. I knew what I did; they knew what I did; God knew what I did. How could I have been so stupid and selfish? I can't believe I did that. So I hid.

It was a retreat from the world; or better yet, an escape from an undeniable coming confrontation with the God of grace. Everything was in the light, and I was naked. So I hid.

But there was no hiding place, only an illusion of an addictive imagination. I was afraid...constantly. Life, the Garden, was no longer a safe place, and I didn't know what to do with that fact. I looked down at myself and saw that I was naked, so I sewed together some fig leaves to cover myself.

But that didn't cover the shame and guilt; they were too itchy, and I never was good with sewing. There were too many gaps, too much airflow. Standing there with my fig leaves, I became aware that I was vulnerable, and that was a threat to my existence.

Perhaps the affair was more than simply moral failure. Perhaps it was a symbol of shattered innocence, that my self-identity had been altered. I was my own worst enemy, and I stole my own innocence. I ate from the other tree, and with it came the horrible truth that nothing would be the same again. So I hid.

I was so preoccupied with self that I was surprised I even heard his whisper: "Where are you? You're supposed to be here with me." I was confronted with the inescapable presence of God. Because his expectation is community and fellowship, his question to me wasn't, "Why did you sin?" That's not the heart of God.

Where are you? That question expresses the arrival of grace; that question lights the match; that question ushers in the warmth of the fire. The heart of the Father is grace, and it is intended to be experienced to the fullest, not simply defined.

Perhaps this is a facet of what is missing in today's church setting: a true understanding and practice of grace.

Light Roast and Bright-Green Buses

I love a good cup of coffee and not with all those silly sweeteners. Although, truth be told, I do enjoy peppermint mocha creamer, But I like my coffee black.

There is a little coffee shop where I live that serves the greatest home-roasted coffee. The beans are roasted right there in the shop, and it smells fantastic. I savor every drop of that coffee.

And the setting is okay. It's small and cramped, with very little seating. If you want to go somewhere where everyone knows your name, this small coffee shop is the perfect location. You will inevitably run into multiple people who will sit with you and talk.

But if you want to study or write a book, don't go to this small coffee shop. So I trade a great cup of coffee for the light roast coffee at Panera Bread. Ah, the light roast. I'm pretty sure its coffee.

I do most of my studying and writing in Panera Bread. In fact, I'm writing this section here at a table facing the front door. And written in Christmas red and green colors is a wonderful sign on the front door that's advertising Toys for Tots. "Partner with Panera Bread and Toys for Tots to Deliver the Message of Hope." Well that's interesting, isn't it? We could deliver hope, which reminds me of one bus ride in Cleveland.

When I was a youth pastor intern, I would often drive to Cleveland on a Saturday to visit a children's ministry. The volunteers would ride bright green buses all over inner-city Cleveland, picking up hundreds of kids from three to eighteen years old. The buses would take them back to a ministry center where there would be fun, music, food, and the message of hope.

Inner-city Cleveland. Most of the children we would pick up were coming from homes of poverty, drugs, alcohol, neglect, and abuse—and I loved those kids. Now I came from a middle-class white suburban churchgoing home, but I loved being on that bus with those kids.

I remember the first time in Cleveland, I thought I would change the lives of these kids. Why? Because I thought I had something they didn't, and I was going to give it to them to make their lives better. But after the first ride with these kids, I realized that they would change me. Which brings us back to the light roast.

I suppose before I even drink that first sip of the light roast, there is some level of expectation. I expect—or better yet, hope—that somehow someway this first sip will be better than the last first sip I had days ago. Hey, Toys for Tots, can you deliver that message of hope?

See, hope is an expectation of things to come. Hope suggests that things can get better. Yet hope wreaks with some stench of discontent, even if small, with the way things are.

If you hope for something, it's because, to some degree, you are discontent with something. How many of you understand that there is no hope in heaven?[4] When you are in that perfect state, at the feet of Jesus, what in the world would you hope for? In the divine state of perfection, there is no need for hope. Hope has already been attained. At the core of hope lies the expectation that what you're experiencing now will ultimately be made better later.

But grace rejoices where you're at right now. Which takes us back to the bus.

I was sitting on the green bus with four middle-class white teenagers. At the very first stop, six young black kids, ranging from three to thirteen years old, climbed on board, each sitting in different seats. A six-year-old girl, however, didn't immediately sit down; she kept walking toward me.

I looked at her, and our eyes locked. She was a beautiful six-year-old with long curly hair with dreads and small white beads at the end of each lock of hair. When she smiled, it revealed the large gap in between her two front teeth. As she came closer, I could smell her hair and clothes as if they were not washed for months.

She stopped right in front of me and said with a lisp, "Hi, thcoot over."

I did. She sat down beside me on her knees facing me. She didn't say a word but leaned over and hugged me so tight as if this was the first hug she received in years. We hugged until it was awkward... for me. I remember thinking through tears, *I'm going to change her by giving her hope.* Little did I know, she would change me by showing me grace. Which takes us back to the light roast.

Coffee is meant to be experienced in its truest form: water filtered through finely ground beans. That's what makes it coffee. When you add all the creamers, sugars, sweeteners, and whip creams, although you can still taste a hint of the coffee, technically, you have changed its form into something else entirely. Black coffee is, in essence, the truest form of coffee.

It is the same with grace. Grace in its truest form is not simply a theological term associated with forgiveness. In Greek, the word is *charis*. At its core, *charis* expresses itself in rejoicing actions through feelings of joy, in the present, as you are. It is an exuberant demonstration of thanksgiving and joy in everyday events. *Charis*, in its essence, is joyfulness.[5] Which takes us back to that bright green bus.

I can't remember her name, but I remember her. During that Saturday, she taught me grace as it was meant to be. She was singing on the bus loudly as we sang popular hip-hop songs. One of the guys I took with me had the song "No Scrubs" by TLC memorized. She loved that. Yet she sang and rejoiced as if she knew nothing else. Some would call that hope, yet she knew what she was going back to: the home life that awaited her after the bright green bus dropped her off. She knew it would be another week before she received another hug, another week before she would be loved. But she sang anyway. She expressed grace as it was meant to be.

I went back the following Saturday by myself, jumped on the same bright green bus and waited in anticipation; she never showed up. I went back the following Saturday on the same bright green bus; she never showed up. For the next five Saturdays, I looked for her. I never saw her again, but she lit that match.

If I listen long enough, I can still hear her voice with the lisp: "No, I don't want no thcrub. A thcrub ith a guy that can't get no love from me. Hangin' out the pathenger thide of my betht friend'th ride, trying to holla at me."[6]

See, when you express grace, you experience deeper levels of grace. When your daily life produces the outcome of exuberant thanksgiving and joy, when you sing loudly regardless of whose listening, when you celebrate life with a dance party in your living room with your spouse and kids, when you laugh more often than you frown, this ushers in the arrival of grace.

Allowing grace to flow from your life is just as vital as receiving grace. Paul says that grace is a free gift from God.[7] We can't earn it, and we don't deserve it. The problem lies when you withhold grace, love, and compassion.

The writer of Lamentations says that God's compassions or mercies are new every morning.[8] The Hebrew word for compassions is *racham*, and it is used thirty-nine times in the Old Testament. Thirty-eight times, it is translated as mercy and compassion. Yet one time it is translated as deeply: "Joseph hurried out for he was deeply stirred over his brother, and he sought a place to weep; and he entered his chamber and wept there" (Genesis 43:30). We see Joseph's affectionate heart for his family as it stirred him to tears.

Perhaps we could say that with Papa God, every morning the affections of his heart are deeply stirred toward his beloved (that would be us), and out of that stirring, grace, mercy, and compassion flood into our lives.

They are new every morning. The root word for new means to restore and renew. It's taking that which has been used up and restoring it to what it was. It's bringing the shine back to the dull places of your heart. Every morning, the heart of our Father is once again deeply stirred toward us, and from that deep affection springs a new grace, a new mercy, and a new compassion.

But what if Papa God distributes his grace and compassion to the level we give it away? "Pay attention to what you hear: with the measure you use, it will be measured to you, and still more will be added."[9] There is a sense that if one decides to daily hoard grace and compassion, the new cannot come. The river of grace that flows from us becomes stopped up, and it begins to pool, and the new doesn't come, and we become bored.

Yet we are expected to be a vessel to extend those new compassions to others in our world. "Be doers of the word, and not hearers only, deceiving yourselves."[10] The grace we experience must be the grace that exits.

I, however, began taking these gifts of new compassions and grace, unwrapping them, taking them out, and placing them on my mantle as trophies. Occasionally I would walk over to them, dust them off, and thank God for giving them to me. Yet they would remain with me. I stopped being grace, compassion, and mercy.

Soon, I began speaking of grace as a definition. Grace became an object, not an experience. The living flow of Jesus became a moldy pool of self. It slowly became all about me. The affair began years before it actually happened.

Maybe we, the church, spend too much time talking about grace. What if we decided to actually light the match?

Very Good

Let's begin in the beginning, shall we?

Throughout the first days of creation, the outcome of God's creation was good. There's a beat, a cadence, a rhythm with the days of creation: it was good, and then it was good, and then it was good.

The Hebrew word for good is *tov*. This word means good, beautiful, something being used for the reason it was created, everything firing on all cylinders. Do you see the picture?

In the English language we would say, "That peach pie is pretty good. The third Godfather movie was pretty good but wasn't as good as the first." Yet in the Hebrew language, the picture deepens to include something working the way it's destined to: the peach pie was *tov*.

In other words, that sliver of peach pie was created to penetrate the depths of my taste buds with deliciousness and satisfaction, causing a sense of serenity and contentment to overwhelm my very existence. It is beautiful. The peach pie wasn't simply good; rather, it completed the reason for which it was created.

God's creation of the universe was *tov*. Everything working the way it was destined to; everything firing on all cylinders; everything so beautiful. Not just once but seven times *tov*[11] (seven is the divine number, the number of perfection). In other words, it's the picture of God's creation being absolutely perfect, not lacking in even the slightest. It was *tov* wholly and completely.

Then the climax of creation: human beings created in the image of their Maker and Savior, and it was very good. It was ***tov mehode***.

Now I need you to grasp the significance of this statement. God created the earth with all the splendor this world holds: mountains, trees, plants, animals, and oceans. The Rockies, the Aspen trees, the sweet corn that is just beginning to ripen, the grandeur of the Himalayas, the crazy anteater, the orange and red sunset that leaves your mouth slightly open in awe.

And if we zoom out: the planets, the moon, the unbelievable color of the nebula, the infinite wonder of the depths of space, the countless galaxies, stars and suns that dwarf our planet, the known and unknown universe that never seems to end.

The splendor and awe of beauty within the universe is *tov*; the artwork painted on the canvas of the universe is *tov*. All of that was simply *tov*. It was good. It was and is working the way it was created to; it's firing on all cylinders. Yet it is simply *tov*.

Yet created humanity was *tov mehode*. Now I want you to pause and breathe that in for a moment. The beauty of the earth, stars, galaxies, nebula are all simply *tov*. But you, my friends, are so much more significant and beautiful; you are *tov mehode*. The pinnacle of all creation; the climax to an already perfect order. The culmination of both divine identity and awestruck wonder. We are *tov mehode*.

At the time of creation, humanity was working the way it was destined to: in a perfect relationship with God, the way it is supposed to be. Imagine going back to Eden. No barriers between you and God; no junk or garbage to separate you from his presence. One day, we will know that again.

But it was *tov mehode*. God created human beings in his image, and it was very good. Yet five chapters later, we find this statement: "The Lord was sorry that he had made man on the earth, and it grieved him in his heart."[12] That's quite a shift, isn't? In five short chapters.

Now, it's vital to understand that the word sorry here does not mean apologetic. It wasn't God saying, "Geez, I'm sorry I made them. How could I have been so stupid. That won't happen again." No. It's *nacham* in Hebrew. It doesn't mean apologetic; it means that it caused him great pain and sorrow to the very core of his heart. It's great anguish in sorrow and mourning. "Oh, my creations, my treasured possessions. They are so far from me. I am *nacham*." The grandeur of his creation now far from him. The "very good" was now "not so good."

So here we have in Genesis 2, a rhythm: it's good, it's good, it's very good. And then five chapters later, it's not so good. Don't we sometimes end the story there? We get this idea that our lives can't get any better. Sometimes we find ourselves in the deepest darkest pit, clawing our way to the top, but never making it. And we have struggles, addictions, hurts, and selfishness that keep us from that perfect relationship with the God who created us the way it was always intended to be: *tov mehode*.

And God is *nacham*; he is in pain, anguish, and mourning at the very core of his heart.

But the story continues: Noah found חן in the eyes of the Lord. This is the very first time this word is used in the Bible. חן is favor, beauty, and grace. But Noah found grace in the eyes of the Lord.

Because the end of one story is the beginning of another, and it begins with grace. It paints the picture of someone stooping in kindness to another. In other words, it paints the picture of a parent-child relationship.

Several years ago, my youngest daughter, Eden, found the markers, and she drew a beautiful colorful arrangement of circles, swirlies, and wavy lines. It was a masterpiece. So beautiful. There was a problem, however; it was on the couch. My wife was not thrilled with her artistic nature. But my wife, in her disappointment, stooped down to wipe the marker off Eden's face—first—even as my daughter held the wet marker in her hand.

That's the Jewish idea of grace; it's a parent-child picture. Grace is about relationship. True grace is about a loving relationship with the God who made us. And God's grace is changing us to become who he already knows we are. My affair left him in pain at the core of his heart, yet his response was and will always be grace.

After the affair, I envisioned a God who was sorry he made me. I imagined him slapping his knee and yelling, "Doggone it, Jeremiah, look what you done did. Now I have to go and whoop ya." I'm not sure why God is from the Kentucky backwoods.

See, my misunderstanding of God shaped the course of my redemption. Because of my misunderstanding, I had swung wide left. I began to try and earn back God's compassion and grace. The next six years of my life was six years full of shame and guilt. It was six years of trying to earn back my assumed standing before God. It was six years of work without an understanding of rest. See, to me, God was still an angry old man from the Kentucky backwoods. I had not yet understood God's goodness that was released from his true identity.

God is our Father. Actually, he is *abba*, which means daddy. This truth never resonated with me until my last trip to Israel. I was in a food store, and from around the corner I heard a young boy, around four to five years old, yell out in a scared voice, "Abba, abba, abba." He was looking for his daddy. I poked my head around the corner just in time for his *abba* to scoop him up in his arms and hug him. The young boy let out a sigh of relief at the same time he said, "*Aaabbaaa*."

That encounter shaped my view of God. He is my daddy. He is my papa. I know that may seem irreverent from some of you, but consider this: Paul writes, "You have received the Spirit of adoption as sons, by whom we cry, 'Abba! Father!'"[13] and "Because you are sons, God has sent the Spirit of his Son into our hearts, crying, 'Abba! Father!' So you are no longer a slave, but a son, and if a son, then an heir through God."[14]

He is not an angry old Gandalf-type figure that stays at a distance watching and waiting for us to mess up, but he is an intimate, close Papa who scoops us up in his arms when we are scared or lost. He is Papa God, our daddy. And until we accept him as so, a true experience of grace will elude us.

When I began expressing my love for him wrapped in acceptance of identity, the natural words that rolled off my tongue became "Papa." My prayers evolved from a puffed-out chest and a deep voice saying, "My heavenly Father," to a man on his knees, through tears crying out, "Abba. Papa." And when my prayers changed, my life changed.

The Abba of grace offers his sons and daughters the fun gift of grace. Even if you have caused him to be *nacham*, he freely covers you with grace as if it's a warm robe right from the dryer.

Rest

Here's a little fun fact: I have no rhythm. Let me clarify. I can clap to a beat, even with flair. I don't want to brag, but people say I'm a pretty good clapper. But if you put me on a dance floor, I'm lost. I suppose I could stand there clapping, but something seems inherently wrong with that. I can't dance. I know what you're thinking: *You can dance if you want to. You can leave this world behind…*

I suppose it's about allowing the rhythm to overwhelm your soul and then releasing that energy into a sweet bust-a-move across the floor. I can master the first part, but when I release that energy, it reminds others of Elaine from Seinfeld.

There's a chemistry, a fluid movement, between two dance partners that captures the very essence of grace. If you watch two people glide across the floor, each step in harmonious rhythm with each other, it intoxicates the depths of your soul. One rhythm; two dance partners; one leads the other. And it captivates you. Hold that thought.

Within every Hebrew name is a story waiting to be told if we but close our eyes and listen. The meaning of Noah's name is found in Genesis 5: "This one shall bring us relief/rest." It comes from the root verb *nuach*, which illustrates the idea of coming to rest after a time of journey, wandering, unrest, and even war. In other words, it's the deep sigh of relief after an intense emotional experience.

It's that moment just after the storm. It's when you hear the words from the doctor, "It's not cancer." It's that moment when your head hits the pillow after being up all night crying and praying that your three-year-old son with asthma would catch his breath, and you hear the normal breathing, and it's that sigh of relief. It's that moment just after you've been fighting and fighting for something or someone, and the sun breaks through; you feel the rays of warmth on your face, and you take that deep breath and say, often times through tears, "It's over."

What does this have to do with grace? Now what's fascinating is that grace in Hebrew is *chen*, spelled *chet-nun* (חן) and just so happens to be the mirror image of Noah's name, *nun-chet* (נח). If grace were to look in the mirror, it would see rest. If rest were to look in the mirror, it would see grace. In other words, there is an intimate connection between rest and grace.

Imagine rest and grace as partners who elegantly dance throughout the ballroom of your life, leading each other through the most difficult decisions and experiences you will ever face. Or better yet, perhaps grace and rest can be most powerfully experienced right smack-dab in the middle of the storm.

Yet, most often, we wait until it's over or there's a pause in the chaos. And the story of "rest" is "grace" saying, "No, no, no. You can experience me now, right where you are…in the midst of chaos, war, unrest, wandering. Before the words 'it's not cancer' are even uttered, rest and grace are available for the taking because Jesus, the essence of grace, powerfully declares from the middle of your storm, 'I will give you rest.'" And it's *tov mehode*.

All for You

The inner voice of Waldorf and Statler hates that truth. It despises the truth that we are very good in the heart of Papa God. The enemy of truth is not lies; the enemy of truth is unbelief. The enemy works issues deep into our lives to contradict that very good identity with God. Unless we seek healing from those issues, we will never reach our ultimate divine identity. It breaks down our usefulness and our influence in this world as we bring in the Jesus movement.

So when I say begin the healing process or seeking healing, I am talking more of the issues we have mentally, spiritually, socially that take root deep down inside of ourselves, realizing that most of these issues come from an awareness of the perception of how we view ourselves. In other words, some, if not most, of these problems that we have deep down in our hearts and souls come from this reality that most of the time we have a very low image of who we are in Christ. Our success in the kingdom of God is determined by our understanding and acceptance of our true identity. Who we believe we are shapes what we do. Far too often, our self-inadequacies get the better of us.

Identity is vital for victory.

Let's explore the divine inner voice that would conquer the feelings of self-inadequacy. The first few verses in the book of John make a foundational statement: "In the beginning was the word, and the word was with God and the word was God. He was with God in the beginning."[15]

Let's understand that Jesus was God even in the beginning. See, there's this false idea that has crept into this world that Jesus was a created being. There are so many cults that try and get Jesus down to their level. If we can make him a created being just like us, then all of that stuff he said throughout the Bible is just pretty neat. He's just an average guy who said some neat things that we can listen to or throw away if we want. So they try and make Jesus one of them—a created being. So John steps in, and in the very first six words of his letter, he announces to the world that Jesus and God are the same. There is no one greater in the universe than Jesus because he is God. That's vital to understand our divine inner voice. It is through this resurrected living Jesus that the voice of truth flows.

Now let's look at the first three words of this first verse: "In the beginning." Where else in Scripture do we see that phrase "In the beginning"? The very first three words of the Hebrew Bible (Genesis 1:1).[16] So we get this idea that even before a single star was created, Jesus was there. Even before the very first act of creation ever happened, Jesus was there with his Father.

The writer continues, "All things were made through him, and without him was not any thing made that was made."[17] So evidently, Jesus had a huge part in the act of creation. Would you agree? If Jesus had not existed "in the beginning," and he was created later on, there would be nothing here. Through Jesus all things were made.

The truth that Jesus was here from the beginning is not just a way of telling us he is God. It goes far deeper than that. Jesus being present at creation reveals a truth that gets to the core of what it means to be human. That there are struggles of identity and belonging that has prevented us from becoming the people that we were destined to become from the beginning. If we hold the truth that Jesus was "in the beginning," then we must accept our divine identity. We must understand the implications of what it means to be created in the image of Papa God. And until we settle into that reality, we will struggle with belonging and self-inadequacy.

And on a deeper level, we struggle with what it means to access the power, inheritance, and authority of Jesus to transform our communities and cities into heaven on earth. Even Jesus prayed to his father, "Your will be done on earth, as it is in heaven."[18] That is our divine calling. That is his expectation for his followers. And that is our greatest struggle. And all creation testifies to grace.

The Image of God

In the beginning, God created humanity in his image. The Hebrew word carries with it the idea of being a representative in physical form, not a carbon copy.[19] Thus, the original "image" represents the rule, reign, authority, and dominion God created humanity to originally possess.

When she was three years old, my oldest daughter, Makiah, loved to see herself in the mirror. When it was time for bed, and we began the long extensive process of bedtime, and she began to brush her teeth, if she couldn't see herself in the mirror, it might as well be the end of the world. She would cry and whine. Her desire was to see herself in the mirror. And when she was done brushing her teeth, she would stare at herself and her beautiful smile, and she asked me every time, "Daddy, am I beautiful?"

"Oh…yes, Makiah. You are beautiful."

I think how wonderful it is that she did that. Yet I often wonder what she saw? Did she see just Makiah? Or did she see the image of God, her Creator? Maybe when Jesus tells us that we need to become like a child, to have the eyes of a child. Maybe it's just that: to look in the mirror and see Jesus, not see a bunch of pimples or baldness or imperfections or everything that you're not, but look and see the image of God, the love, grace, and peace of your Creator.

In the letter of James, he writes, "Do not merely listen to the word and deceive yourself, do what it says." I had a mentor whose favorite thing to say was, "Does what you believe equal what you do? Because if I watch what you do, I will know what you believe."[20] Belief and action are inseparable. A right belief will guide a right action. How you treat others and yourself is governed by what you believe about the beginning.

James continues to write, "Anyone who listens to the word but does not do what it says is like a man who looks at his face in the mirror and forgets what he looks like."[21]

What's interesting is that in the original Greek text there is a word, *geneseos*,[22] that was written to describe the face. Yet the NIV translation leaves that out of their version of the Bible. The ESV will translate this word as "natural," but that doesn't seem to do it justice. It comes from the root word genesis…or "the beginning."

Now let's read it properly: "Anyone who listens to the word but does not do what it says is like a man who looks at his *genesis* face in the mirror and forgets what he looks like." His genesis face; his beginning face. Maybe it's the idea that when he looks into the mirror, or looks into God's word, he is supposed to see the image of what he was in the beginning.

What if James is talking about our image from the beginning, our destiny in Jesus Christ, our purpose as Christians in this world? It is our image from the beginning or our first face, the perfect reflection of God. But along the way, humanity screwed it up, distorted the image. What if the Bible is a love story showing us how to restore that first image to reflect the true essence of Jesus?

When James wrote his letter, there were people in the church who would come and listen to the rabbi, sing the chants and hymns, recite the prayers; but when they left the church, they would continue to do the things they had always done before: lie, cheat, steal, cuss out the person who cut them off with their donkey. That doesn't sound like today, does it? There wouldn't be change of heart; action wouldn't be stirred by belief.

So in essence, James is saying, "If you come to church and do what Christians do, but then leave and do what the rest of the world does, don't call yourself Christians. You're making it harder for the rest of us."

Some of you might be clapping and some of you might be saying, "Boy that's harsh," but that's what I love about the book of James.

Now I'm not pointing fingers and holding my head high; I'm guilty of this too. But how many of us say, "I am so thankful for God's love" or we sing about God's love with our hands held high, but when we are confronted by that person who annoys us or is a little different than we are, love takes a back seat. Or if we do something wrong to someone else, maybe we point fingers or make excuses, and we don't take the first step in making amends. Or what about justice? How many of us know that Jesus desires us to take care of the orphans and the widows, the homeless, the poor, but when was the last time we did that hands on with hands dirty?

In 2009, I was part of a team that established a gathering of youth pastors and young adult pastors in our denomination from all over the United States. The purpose was to initiate the justice of God through ministry in our areas. We all gathered together in Colorado Springs. We had a few hours for sightseeing. I took four pastors on a mission to get to the top of Pike's Peak. As we drove down Route 24, we began to notice that alongside the road in a ravine, there were hundreds of people in a homeless community living in tents in the Rocky Mountains in winter.

Our van went silent. We just looked and felt God stirring our hearts. Yet as we passed this community of hurting people, somebody said, "I wonder if Pikes Peak will be open?" And we continued on our journey. We did nothing about it.

My heart still hurts. It's almost as if I looked in the mirror and saw what I was supposed to be, the image of God expressing the love and justice of Jesus, but immediately forgot what I looked like. James says, "If you call yourself a Christian, but you don't do anything about it, what's the point?"

That's what I love about James. Is it harsh? Absolutely, but it keeps me focused on what I am destined to reflect: the justice, love, grace, mercy, and peace of God—or better yet, reflect Jesus himself. Redeemed humanity must come to the realization that our souls ought to be a reflection of God's goodness.

The Exodus, His Exodus, and My Exodus

After Adam and Eve relinquished their divine image, the following generations found themselves in quite a pickle. Egypt, the new superpower, had enslaved the Hebrew people and built its empire on their backs.

I can imagine their longing for freedom, how they would share stories of God's miraculous works with the previous generations.

…how there used to be a garden where man and God walked and talked.

…how there was a great flood that destroyed the world, but God saved eight.

…how God brought up Abraham, Isaac and Jacob.

…how Joseph was sold into slavery by his own brothers, yet God redeemed and rescued him to become the second most powerful man in Egypt.

And now—being whipped, beaten, starved, forced to carry bricks—their lives were overflowing with affliction, misery, oppression, depression, and bondage. In their eyes, Egypt wasn't just another country; it became a "land of slavery and bondage." For future generations who found themselves in any bondage, slavery, or affliction, they would simply say, "Oh, you're in Egypt." And that would summon up the imagery, feelings, and experiences of their time in slavery. I can imagine their longing for the day they would experience their ultimate redemption. Life was so good, but now it's not, yet a day will come.

So God's people are living in the land of darkness, slavery, hurt, sorrow, misery, addiction, guilt, low self-esteem, feeling ignored, hopelessness, being uncared for and unloved. Can anyone relate?

And God steps and says,

> I have surely seen the affliction of my people who are in Egypt and have heard their cry because of their taskmasters. I know their sufferings, and I have come down to deliver them out of the hand of the Egyptians and to bring them up out of that land to a good and broad land, a land flowing with milk and honey.[23]

Papa God sees our hurt and hears our cries. The Hebrew word for cries is *tsa'aqah*. It's the expression of pain, the hurt, the misery, the sound that comes from our mouths when we are wounded. But ancient rabbis also believed that *tsa'aqah* was a question: "Did anybody see that? Who will come to my rescue? Am I alone?"[24]

And their cry is what ignited a new passion for a new story in their lives. Their cries were founded on their hopelessness. Their cries were rooted in feeling unloved. And their cries are what stirred the heart of God. See, Papa God doesn't just hear their cries; he does something about it. And God leads them on an exodus. It was change; it was a journey of reclamation; it was a journey of restoration; it was a journey of hope.

That's when the journey of restoration actually happens. When you reach the end of your rope, and you cry out—not casually, but deep within your heart—the *tsa'aqah* of hope, that's when it begins. When everything falls apart; when you are confronted by your powerlessness; when you truly admit that your life is unmanageable; when there's nothing left to do but cry out in our desperation, oppression, hurt, and misery. God hears our cries. God hears our questions, and he leads us on our own exodus, our exodus toward restoration. Because restoration demands hope.

The world is fueled by hope. The moment people stop believing that it could get better is the moment that all is lost. Hope is the engine that drives humanity toward a better future. It's as if all humanity has some sort of "first face," and if our lives are not on the road to reclaim it, hope kicks in and forces us to believe. Living in a place of despair, hopelessness, and bondage is not our first instinct. We were created for the Garden life, a place of peace, grace, and joy with our Creator. That is our first best destiny.[25]

Jesus illustrates this with a great story of a son[26] who has it good, all that he can ever want. But he leaves home, searching for what he believes to be his destiny. He takes an early inheritance and ends up living in a distant land, which is not Israel, working for a citizen of that land, who is not Jewish. So in essence, this man decides to leave his identity and self-worth behind as he enters a land of bondage, a land of addictions, a land of oppression and depression, a land of misery and affliction. Or you could say, if you were Jewish, he went to live in "Egypt," and that one word would describe all the issues that he faced.

I was in "Egypt" once. I left home, squandered my inheritance on things that I believed made me feel good about life. I lived in a distant land of despair, hopelessness, and oppression. I was stuck; to say I was in a rut would be an understatement. This was a chasm, and I willfully walked into it. With the affair, I surrendered the goodness of the Garden life. I yielded my first best destiny.

And just as the son in the story, I woke up to myself eating pig slop. How did I end up here? Why in the world did I think this would be better? How could I have done that? It was so much better before…Isn't it amazing how we can walk away from God's purposes and direction and then wonder why it went so bad? I suppose we could chalk it up to human nature, or perhaps a misunderstanding of our "first face."

And I am willing to guess that most of us are living there to some degree. All of us have given up some part of our divine identity, some aspect of our "first face." All of us have some kind of ties to a distant land, the land of darkness. Some of us live there, some of us travel back and forth, and some of us straddle the edge.

But just like the younger son, our inner voices prevent us from leaving that dark distant land. So we must change, and hope is our key to change.

Sometimes we are afraid to change even if our past was painful. We resist even thinking about change because of our fear of the unknown. It's saying, "I guess I'll give this a shot." That's not openness; that's fear. An openness to change is not just scratching the surface. But it's a movement deep, deep within your heart, mind, and soul that cannot stand to do this anymore. It's that burning in the pit of your heart that ignites a fire to change.

Change is successful when truth moves from an idea to a conviction. It's what I call "the most difficult eighteen-inch move ever"… from your head to your heart. It's not saying, "Boy, I wish I could stop this affair," or "I really wish I could stop drinking," or "I just would really like it if I didn't view myself as an accident, or ugly, or fat, or worthless, or unloved. I mean I tried stopping ten times but couldn't." Have you ever heard that? That is not an openness to change; that's an "I'm not sure I really want to change."

Now I have never experienced firsthand the power of the addiction to cigarettes or alcohol, but I have witnessed the miraculous power of the risen Jesus over those things. I have experienced how Jesus can take a person who doesn't say, "I wish I could," but rather, through tears and sorrow, cries out from the depths of their heart, "Papa God, I need your power, your hope" as a fire ignites a movement within their lives. God will honor that person. That's an openness to change.

It was a cold February in 2011. The affair had ended, but I was eating the pig slop of self-loathing, guilt, shame, and despair, most of which I would wrestle with for the next six years. In January, I had resigned as a pastor, but I had forgotten to give my keys back to the church. So on this cold February night, I looked up from my pig slop and wondered how I got here. I couldn't believe this is where I was.

I went to the church. I walked down the aisle of that gym and walked to the front of the stage. I remember being like that son, shaking and crying, saying, "I am no longer worthy to be your son. I wonder if he will take me back. I hope he takes me back." I knelt down sobbing through tears and snot pouring out of my face, barely able to catch my breath—a picture of desperation. I asked for forgiveness. It's interesting, now I have the understanding, that even then while I was a long way off, the Father saw me, felt compassion, and ran and embraced me. Just like that son in the story.

In the story, the father was so joyful that his son returned that he said, "'Bring the fattened calf and kill it, and let us eat and celebrate. For this my son was dead, and is alive again; he was lost, and is found.' And they began to celebrate."

I imagine that's how it was for me and for you, for all of us who lived, at any length, in "Egypt," who woke up eating the slop and who came to their senses and recognized their "first face." He cries out to his father for mercy, and his father gives him restoration. His exodus was a journey of restoration. It was God leading him back to what he had always intended him to be. That's hope. And that's what God wants to do with you and me.

True healing from all the junk and garbage in our lives cannot truly take place unless hope takes precedence. Are you ready to begin a new journey, a new exodus, a new hope? Are you ready for the fat cow?

Names

There is something in medieval literature used to describe the majesty, divinity, glory, and humanity of Jesus at the same time: the mandorla. Imagine two intertwining circles: one representing heaven, the perfection, the glory of the divine; and the other representing earth, the imperfection of humanity. One representing perfection, the other imperfection.

What's fascinating is the little section where the two intertwine. That section is labeled as Jesus. Why? Because it is the ultimate representation of perfection inhabiting an imperfect world. He is the God-man: fully God as if he were not man at all, yet fully human as if he were not God at all. It's okay, I don't understand it either. But the mandorla is these two worlds colliding. So throughout the Bible is this tension between these worlds: heaven and earth, God's rule and reign and our rule and reign, perfection and imperfection.

In Genesis 1, there is a perfect creation where things were as God intended them to be. In the last book of the Bible, Revelation, there is a recreation where things will be as God intends them to be. So the Bible begins with this ideal place, this perfect place, and it ends with a perfect, ideal place. Not only that, but it begins with an image of who we are supposed to be, and it ends with how we are going to be.

But now we have this chunk of time between Genesis and Revelation called life, and we are in it right now. And for most of us, if not all of us, there are parts of our lives that doesn't quite line up with that "first face" image. So in our lives, there is this tension between the ways things are and the way things ought to be.

It's funny how you can look back on certain times in your life and see the reality of goodness that was present. Yet when you are going through it, the goodness seems to be invisible. You create a perception of what you believe life should become, and that perception actually becomes antireality. And in that atmosphere of antireality, tension's seed is planted. Discontentment begins to blossom.

I should probably pause for a moment and say that I always had this sense, deep in my heart and soul, that something greater for me and Elisha was around the corner. Not something better, but rather some sort of journey that God would manifest his greatness through us, something where God was about to display his glory and power through us.

It's the idea of Christmas coming. How excited you get when the snow starts to fly, the music begins to play, the decorations emerge. There is an anticipation of the excitement of Christmas. Each day that comes is one day closer to Christmas. Something great is coming one day at a time. And the closer and closer you get to Christmas, you realize they keep pushing Christmas back a month. It's that anticipation of something coming yet never arriving.

This is the sense that I have always had in my life. Get ready; it's coming! But years would march on, and that thing that I knew was going to happen never would. Soon, I began expecting it wouldn't happen. I didn't even know what it was, but I believed it wasn't coming.

Rather than waiting on Papa God for his arrival, I began to pursue that thing on my own. In 2003–2008, I was an associate pastor in a church that loved me, with a senior pastor who treated me like a son, in one of the greatest hunting grounds in the nation. And I was confused because it wasn't coming. I was frustrated that my life was not flowing the way I thought it should. So in 2007, I began looking for a way to bring it. In 2008, I left that place in pursuit of contentment.

Leaving Pennsylvania to pursue an antireality left me even more skewed in my thinking. I began to rely more on self than on Papa God.

When I had left the church in Pennsylvania, this internal tension assaulted my emotions and thoughts constantly. I had moved from an atmosphere where I had incredible accountability and became an associate pastor in another church where I had zero accountability. The voice of Statler and Waldorf morphed into a new heckle with that move. They began to loudly taunt, "You deserve better. You deserve something different. Everyone says how amazing you are, and they are right! You're great. Show them how great you are." Pride, arrogance, and egotism found their place on center stage in my life. This was it, and it feels good. But worldly pleasures soon fade.

When antireality becomes normal, it often becomes boring. You begin trying to find other ways to feed the selfish soul. When your life isn't grounded on the goodness of Papa God, doors are left wide open, and Satan can walk right through them. The tension between the way things were and the way they ought to be waged a war in my head. I imagine it's the same with some of you.

So within life as we know it, there is this tension between what is and what ought to be. Tension between heaven and earth; tension between perfection and imperfection. But God is a God who is calling and drawing us closer and closer to become the people we were destined to be. So this life then becomes, not a waiting room for the future heaven, but it becomes a battleground to reclaim your "first face."

Now bear with me (I promise this will make sense at the end of this section), but have you ever made a decision to read the Bible through cover to cover? Yeah, I have too. I've done it numerous times, and I'm sure you have too. Have you ever gotten to a boring section and skipped over it? C'mon, I know you have. Like Genesis 5? Genesis 5 is a list of names and ages—that's it. Just a name and how old he was when he died. But chapter six is Noah's flood, so we skip five to get to six. Boring genealogy, but I do want to say that it's in here for a reason. And if we skip it, we miss something spectacular.

Now in Genesis 4, an ugly thing happened with Cain and Abel. They were brothers who just didn't get along, so Cain murdered his brother. Ugly and evil, it's earth as he intended it to be. So chapters one and two are about this perfect creation that God intended for us to live. Ideal, as it should be, with a perfect "first face" from God.

In chapter 3, man decided they knew what was best for their own lives, and that ideal image and relationship with God was broken. In chapter 4, the first murder took place. The earth is becoming more and more as man intended it to be.

So do you sense the tension in this story? Between heaven and earth; a tension between the circles. Are you sensing the need for restoration and healing? Because all the sudden, chapter 4 ends with a phrase: "At that time men began to call on the Lord." At that time men began to call on the Lord. At what time? The death of Abel? The birth of a new son Seth? Or was it at the time when people began to realize that their image was broken? Did they begin to realize that something didn't line up? Did they begin to understand that what was perfect and whole and complete would forever be burned into their hearts and souls? There was something deep within them, a burning and longing to return to what was their "first face." And so they cried out.

Welcome chapter five. It's the genealogy from Adam to Noah. Let me just write them here: Adam, Seth, Enosh, Kenan, Mahalalel, Jared, Enoch, Methuselah, Lamech, and Noah. Let me remind you that in ancient times, names meant something—names were valuable. Back then, your mom and dad would name you because the meaning of your name would mean something. It would describe a circumstance in which you were born or your divine destiny.

Today, we name our children something that simply sounds good. Oh, how I wish we would recover that aspect of naming. My name is Jeremiah, meaning "may Jehovah exalt." Yes please, he certainly may.

Names mean something. Here we have ten names, each meaning something different. Let me show you the meaning here: Adam is "man." Seth means "appointed." Enosh means "mortal." Kenan is "sorrow" (I wonder what happened when Kenan was born). Mahalalel is from two Hebrew words: *mahalal* meaning "praise" and *el* meaning "one true God." Jared means "shall come down." Enoch means "teaching or training." Methuselah comes from two Hebrew words: *muth* meaning "death" and *shalach* meaning "shall bring" (it was his death that brought the flood of Noah). Lamech means "powerful." And Noah is "rest."

Names mean something. Powerful names. So at the end of chapter 4, smack dab in the middle of this tension between what was and what is, smack dab in the middle of this tension between the perfect image of God we were destined to have and the image we were creating for ourselves, comes these cries from the people—at that time men began to call upon the Lord.

Then Genesis 5 comes along with a list of powerful names, a genealogy of sorts. But what if this genealogy is something more? What if it isn't just names, but what if it is a direct response to the cries of the people? What if God wanted them and wanted us to understand that something was going to happen later that would bring heaven and earth together? What if this list of names tells a story of what is to come? What if it's a story of healing and restoration? The center of the mandorla filled in completely and wholly.

> Man…appointed…mortal…sorrow…praise one true God…shall come down…teaching…death shall bring…powerful…rest.

I'll let you catch your breath for a second. The genealogy is a message of hope, a message of redemption, a message of restoration and healing. It's God saying, "There is an ideal image of yourself, your 'first face,' but you screwed it up. You messed it up. Your life is filled with junk and garbage and sin, but there is someone coming who will restore it all."

His name is Jesus: the perfect image of God, showing you and me how to live a whole and complete life, showing us how to be restored and healed to God. The perfection of heaven meeting the imperfect world, and restoring it.

And Jesus has come to show us how to live a full and complete life, a life better than we have ever dreamed possible. He has come so that we would recognize our true image—the image of love, grace, mercy, peace, and goodness—extending those things to the world around us. It's God's ultimate sign of grace to this broken world.

There is a person who we already are in God's eyes, created in his image. And our journey of faith is learning to live like this is true. Jesus loves you and wants to pull you into his divine purposes. Jesus loves you exactly as you are but loves you too much to let you stay there. His desire is that every day you take one step closer to becoming the person he has intended you to be. A reclamation of your "first face," your first best destiny.

* * * * *

The essence of grace is displayed in the essence of Jesus. He is ushering us into a new paradigm of living. Life is not simply living; life is living simply with the divine mission to reclaim that which was lost.

Grace commissions us to embark on that adventurous journey of faith. Grace sets our sail on the new horizons of hope. Grace is the courage to climb the mountains of anxiety and fear with reckless abandon. And though exhausted, we are empowered by grace to plant our flag at the summit in victory.

Grace encourages the soul to explore new worlds in search of its first best destiny. And when you find it, grace takes your hand and pulls you along in relentless pursuit. Grace enables you to fall on your knees in thanksgiving and joy saying, "God, I can't believe I get to live this life."

Wake up! Your journey, your expedition, your exodus, your quest has come. May grace set your face to the challenge and may grace bring you victory.

Celebration

Celebration is a confrontation, giving attention to
the transcendent meaning of one's actions.

—Abraham Heschel

Essence of Celebration

I do love the story of the Exodus. God's people found themselves in slavery, bondage, misery, and affliction from the superpower of their day, Egypt. God's promise to Jacob, that his descendants would be as numerous as the dust on the earth, had finally come to fruition.

There were so many Hebrews that the Egyptians began to worry that their way of life may be threatened. They had erected this empire, and now they had to keep it by any means necessary. So the Egyptians enslaved the Hebrew people; they were forced to produce bricks to build storehouses. Yet the Hebrew people continued to multiply. So the Egyptians forced greater labor upon them, which, in turn, allowed the Hebrew people to multiply even more.[27]

Funny isn't it? You can force a man into doing slave labor making bricks the entire day; being whipped, stripes of blood across his back; being spit on, mocked and ridiculed; and when he's done for the day, knowing that tomorrow will be just the same or even worse. Yet he will still go home to his wife and have sex.

There's something powerful in that. Sex is an intimate act between two people whom God unites together. The movement of sex beckons the divine unity that was established before the foundation of the world. And for those slaves, it was a time to forget the pain and celebrate normality and feel free.

Nevertheless, the Hebrew population grew. The new pharaoh of Egypt decided that death would be the way to slow down the population growth. He made a decree to throw every Hebrew newborn into the Nile River.[28] And they did. All except one—Moses, the deliverer of Israel, the hero which the rest of Scripture embodies.

Through a series of miraculous events, Moses leads his people to freedom. Now place yourself into the situation: slavery, depression, hopelessness, misery, affliction, oppression, bondage, you're whipped, beaten, spit on, verbally abused, emotionally molested, and physically beaten for generations. And now you're free. You walk out those gates away from the empire that enslaved you smiling, laughing, and crying. What would you think of the good news of freedom? What does deliverance feel like to you? What does celebration look like to you?

The word for celebrate is *chagag*. It paints the picture of dancing, feasting, joyful movement, and it also is the word for circle. A circle represents cycles or seasons. The death of winter is always followed by the life of spring, where green buds and beautiful flowers emerge. Yet that is followed by a death, where those same green buds begin their descent to earth as brown brittle leaves. Yet a few months later, those same green buds emerge. A circle represents the endless cycle of seasons.

Yet it also represents a progression. All of creation is progressing somewhere. It's impossible to look out at creation and see a static environment. Contained within creation is a movement. It's all headed somewhere.

Hence, within the picture of the circle, there's a movement from dark to light, from death to life, from mourning to joy. Celebration then becomes an embrace of the circle. The essence of *chagag* is the understanding that all of life is a movement headed somewhere. It's the understanding that life has purpose and ultimately progressing toward light, life, and joy.

Yet, most often, our celebration begins after darkness, death, and mourning pass. We celebrate the after. We find joy in the after, so we say things like, "After this is all over, then I can breathe again," or "I can't wait until this is over, then I can heal," or "When this passes, then it's back to normal." Celebration then becomes a feeling only secondary to the pain. Once you feel good, then you can celebrate. But *chagag*, the circle, says there's something better around the corner. You may be in darkness, death, and mourning; but hold on tight, it's not over yet. Light, life, and joy are coming.

Chagag is first used in Exodus 12[29] when God commands his people to celebrate the coming freedom. He told them to celebrate what was to come. "Your freedom is on the way; celebrate now with the promise of freedom." See, the essence of celebration comes not with the act of freedom, but the promise of freedom. We learn to celebrate with the promise.

All creation is progressing to something better, so we celebrate with that promise. We can dance, feast, make joyful movements even in the dead of winter—even when we are smack dab in the middle of the most difficult time in our lives. It is there the promise of the circle takes shape.

Expectation

Expectation is a funny thing. The least of it will allow impossibility, yet an overabundance ushers in discontent. It's one of those things in life that you need, but in the right dose. Expectation can lead you to a better future, or it could leave you speechless with feelings of discontent, disappointment, and ultimately, hopelessness.

The key to expectation is patience. If you are a follower of Jesus, it's an understanding of his timing versus your timing. We receive a promise from God, and our timing initiates a countdown to fulfillment.

The problem is, that countdown doesn't exist in the spiritual realm. Rather, he will give you a promise that most of the time you must grow into. Some of my prophetic promises are accompanied by the understanding that quite a bit of shaping must occur in my life.

The promise is there, but it must be claimed. In other words, the prophetic promise to lead a new movement of young people sensitive to the Spirit of God, who teaches and shapes their generation, will not be accomplished by sitting on the couch playing Xbox One.

If you were given a promise from God, a prophetic promise, and it hasn't come to fulfillment yet, most likely there's some more growing and shaping that must happen in your life. So you wait for greater things.

I stated earlier that I knew God's movement of power was coming in my life, that a greater thing was around the corner, yet I wasn't patient and refused to wait on him. I didn't realize it then, but that expectation of greater things began to flood in my life when I married Elisha. Our union ignited the fuse for an arrival of a divine destiny etched in time before the world began. This divine destiny of greater things in our lives was dependent on waiting for Papa God to usher us there.

In the book of Luke, the author tells the story of the birth of Jesus. Within this story, the author loads in tons of tension and conflict. Luke writes that the Roman Caesar decided to have a census and registration of each person in their hometown. Luke then writes an interesting line: Joseph went to Bethlehem "because he was of the house and lineage of David."[30]

It's just a subtle line but packed full of expectation and promise. The line of David suggests prestige and honor. It's the status that comes with dropping names. "You remember David, only the greatest king ever to have lived and reigned in Israel. You know, a man after God's own heart. Yeah, well, funny thing…I'm in his line. No big deal, but you know—" Joseph drops mic and walks away. You get the idea. Joseph's inheritance is kingly.

Luke goes on to write that Mary gave birth to her firstborn son.[31] The firstborn always had the right to the throne. This is the author's way of saying that this baby is in line to be the next king. So in these couple of verses, we already see that this baby has a very high status, a sense of kingly honor. It's a sense that this kid has got it. He's the one, the chosen one. This is it. Finally, our king has come.

Expectations always come from presuppositions. Your culture, land, language, and experiences all dictate how you perceive and understand something. Unless you have experience with sheep, watching them act and behave, you will never have a full understanding of Jesus as your shepherd.

Your experiences shape how you understand something; how you understand something shapes your expectations. This first-century world had always been ruled by a king, and God made some prophetic promises to these people about the ultimate king who would be coming. Their expectation stemmed from an understanding that the right king would change everything.

Yet the author writes that Mary wrapped him in cloths and placed him in a manger.[32] Why? Because there was no room in the inn. This future king, the chosen one, can't find a room at the inn? There's always room for a future king. And placed him in a manger, a feeding trough? That doesn't make any sense. A woman who is ready to be wed to someone in the line of the greatest king ever to have lived has to give birth to a kingly baby and place him in a manger?

Already, the author upsets the entire known order of things. In between the Old and New Testaments, there are four hundred years. During these four hundred years, they waited for the next David. They were waiting and expecting someone from the line of David to free them to become who they were destined to be.

The Jews were miserable. They were conquered, oppressed, and polluted. Hope was running low, faith was even lower. They were convinced that now the only thing that could save them and their faith was the appearance of the Messiah.

And during these 400 years you would unroll the Isaiah scroll and read Isaiah 9:6–7:

> For to us a child is born, to us a son is given; and the government shall be upon his shoulder, and his name shall be called Wonderful Counselor, Mighty God, Everlasting Father, Prince of Peace. Of the increase of his government and of peace there will be no end, on the throne of David and over his kingdom, to establish it and to uphold it with justice and with righteousness from this time forth and forevermore.

Someone is coming! He will free us from our oppressors! He will destroy the Roman government. He will bring us back to our first best destiny. We can't wait.

And you would excitedly roll out the Jeremiah scroll where in 23:5–6 it says,

> Behold, the days are coming, declares the Lord, when I will raise up for David a righteous Branch,

and he shall reign as king and deal wisely, and shall execute justice and righteousness in the land. In his days Judah will be saved, and Israel will dwell securely. And this is the name by which he will be called: "The Lord is our righteousness."

That's what they longed for; that's what they desired above all. To be taken from this land of darkness into the land of light. They would wait and tell stories and dream together of what could be, of their expectations of the coming one.

Where is the king? But there also has to be some hesitation, hasn't there? Because so far, all the other kings didn't really do a bang-up job. They didn't really succeed, did they?

If I'm living at this time, somewhere in the back of mind I'm thinking, *Kings use war to bring peace. Kings raise and collect taxes to pay for soldiers to use for war to bring peace. Kings use slaves to build larger kingdoms and walls to protect himself from war. With earthly kings come the expected unrest that leads to a so-called better peace.*

So there has to be some hesitation. Yes there is coming a king to bring us freedom, but at what cost? How much war will there be? How high will the taxes get? Will I be a slave for this coming king? Questions and hesitation, yet still an expected longing for something better.

So you see the tension in the first few verses. And that's exactly what the author wants you to feel: tension between expectation of a promise and expectation of reality.

The author goes on to explain that there were a group of shepherds in the area.[33] But these were not some random group of shepherds living out in the middle of the desert somewhere. Most scholars believe they were in charge of raising the sacrificial lambs used for temple worship. These shepherds were charged with tending the lambs that would be killed during temple sacrifices.[34]

It's ironic that because of their jobs, they were considered unclean, which means that they could not be a part of temple worship. They raised the lambs for sacrifice but could not participate at all. They were outcasts in charge of the single most important thing on the face of the planet at that time. Isn't that a slap in the face?

For the four hundred years between the Old and New Testaments, generations of shepherds have raised these lambs never expecting to be a part of anything miraculous at all. Day after day, doing the same old thing, being treated the same old way, they settled into the ordinary, average life. It could be said that their expectation was firmly planted in reality.

In the movie *Old School*, Will Ferrell plays a married, forty-something-year-old suburban man who finds himself at a college party. Somebody in the party offers him a drink of alcohol. He turns it down by saying, "I have a big day tomorrow."

They ask him, "A big day doing what?"

He responds, "Well, um…actually it's a pretty nice little Saturday. We're gonna go to Home Depot, buy some wallpaper, maybe get some flooring, stuff like that. Maybe Bed Bath and Beyond, I don't know. I don't know if we'll have enough time…"

Do you remember the scene? Everyone I talked to remembers it. Why? It's funny. But it's so much more than going to Home Depot on a Saturday. The man is bored. He has the life that so many people call the American Dream. He has a wife, a house, a job, security, comfort, freedom, opportunity, yet it has left him feeling bored, numb, in a certain state of despair. His so-called "success" has provided a distraction from just how deeply unsatisfied he is with his life.

One author says, "If we aren't careful, our success and security and abundance can lead to a certain sort of boredom, a numbing predictability, a paralyzing indifference that comes from being too comfortable."[35]

So here are the shepherds doing what they always have done, perhaps expecting nothing but the next day. In a sense, being content with being discontent. The story begins with the shepherds doing what they have always done. But one day, that all changes. An angel appears and begins a new narrative in their hearts. They would find a baby, the future king, wrapped in swaddling clothes. Wait, that's what shepherds do. Do you mean we're going to find this future king, not wrapped in purple silk, but itchy scratchy clothes? That's weird.

The angel goes on to say that you will find the baby lying in a manger. Wait a sec, that's what shepherds use. You mean, we're not going to find him born in a palace? He's going to be lying in the same thing that we use to feed the sacrificial lambs? That's weird.

Can you begin to sense the tension within the shepherds? Can you begin to sense their curiosity? Can you begin to feel the joy and excitement that is rising within them, when they start thinking, *Unbelievable. He is just like us. Maybe this king will be different. Maybe this king will bring a different kind of peace. Maybe this king will be the Savior of our souls.*

After the angel speaks, they return praising God. The story begins with the shepherds doing what they have always done. The story ends with the shepherds returning to their fields, glorifying and praising God. The story begins with the mundane and ordinary events of life, those things that leave you with a sense of boredom and monotony, an ordinary expectation of reality. Yet the story ends with the extraordinary making a journey back to the place where it all began.

The story begins and ends in the same physical location. The difference is the awareness of exactly what you've been missing all along. The difference is the expectation that what you've been searching for your whole life has been right in front of your eyes the whole time.

The author continues that Mary pondered all of this in her heart. Pondered what? I have the future king in front of me, but he's lying in a manger, with itchy clothes, being visited by the poor, smelly social outcasts known as shepherds. This doesn't quite line up. Why? Because Jesus isn't typical. Jesus isn't mundane. Jesus isn't average. The moment that we stop expecting to be a part of something greater is the moment when we find ourselves expecting the least.

This story of Jesus is about expectations. It's about realigning how you see the world. It's about waking up and realizing that Jesus wants to heal our hearts and souls and allowing him to do the miraculous. It's about taking all of this and pondering it over and over and over in your heart, hoping and praying that God allows you to fully experience everything he has in store for you. It's about the expectation of the promise.

Passover

People ask me to describe the moment God rescued me. I think they are expecting a story about a golden beam of light appearing out of the heavens, illuminating me in glory; angels appearing; and the voice of God thundering something about sheep, fiery wheels, and forgiveness. So when I tell them that there were no lights, no angels, no voice—that there was just me, an empty room, and an almost unnoticeable voice in the depths of my heart—I see them deflate. They wanted a miraculous story that would leave them in wonder, and what I gave them was a miraculous story that left me in wonder.

The miracle is always more powerful when it involves yourself. The stories of our personal exodus are filled with wonder and awe as we remember our journey to freedom. When we read our testimony to my two girls, they journeyed with us to freedom. They wept when we wept, laughed when we laughed. Our journey became their journey.

When impossibility emerges in their life, they will remember the miracle of their mom and dad's story. They will remember how their dad was a slave, how he was in depression and self-hate, yet how Papa God met him in a dark empty room and led him to freedom through a wide-open sea, how he chose redemption. They will remember how their mom was so hurt, how she daily wept, yet how she entered into the presence of Papa God and chose forgiveness. And they will celebrate that journey to freedom.

To this day, the Jewish people celebrate their past and present journey from being slaves in Egypt to heirs of the Promised Land. I say present journey because, to the Jewish mind, the past is always applied to the present. Truth knows no boundaries. To deliver his people, God sent ten plagues to persuade Pharaoh to give his people freedom. Pharaoh ignored each plague, ultimately bringing the final plague of death to the firstborn child.[36]

To save his people, God commanded them to sacrifice a perfect lamb and wipe its blood on the doorposts of their house. In doing so, he would pass over their homes and spare their child.[37] This final act allowed Pharaoh to release God's people into their freedom.

With this act, God gave his people a command to celebrate a feast where they were to eat and remember. They were to eat this meal in haste, *khippazon*, which means hurry, alarm, and trepidation. It's the defining moment of the first fast food.

Anyway, the symbolic representation of *khippazon* was not the physical means of eating, but rather the importance of the attitude in which they ate. Originally, the first Passover was not to be a celebratory feast where the people were indifferent to the suffering happening outside their homes. Rather, the first Passover was to be consumed with *khippazon* since their freedom was redeemed with an immense cost to human and animal life.[38] Their freedom was given. God took a people in slavery and redeemed their lives.

So in essence, we could say that Passover in the Old Testament represents a movement, a passing from negative to positive, a celebration of expectation of what is to come. Passover is not a static, complacent celebration of a historical event, but a continual active understanding that God is redeeming and restoring his people and this world.

Passover stems from the understanding that God has done this in the past yet expecting that he will do it in the future. Passover is not defined by time; it is a past, present, and future event all at the same time, yet all distinctly different.

The Passover celebration is about a defeat and death, yet it discovers the redemption and grace of this world. It remembers the bitterness, the tears, and the oppression of slavery in Egypt, yet it embodies the joy and celebration that accompanies the liberation with the Exodus.

Jesus celebrated Passover throughout his life. His last supper was a celebration of this feast. He broke bread and drank wine as a way to illustrate his death. So, at its core, Passover remembers the broken body, spilled blood, and gruesome death of Jesus, yet it portrays the hope and good grace of the resurrected Messiah. As such, Passover declares not only the remembrance of past events, but a vision of love, grace, and hope for the future manifested through the presence of Jesus.

This is the Lord's Supper, or communion, or Eucharist, or Passover. To celebrate the Lord's Supper is to recognize the outpouring of good grace and not only react introspectively, but initiate an avenue to bless humanity with good grace. It is a movement to cultivate the beauty of grace. It is a movement that ought to bring all humanity into the fellowship and participation with good grace.

See, when one celebrates the bread and wine, the only natural progression is the blessing of fellow humanity. Passover has, at its core, a rhythm and cadence that projects the continual movement from which all humanity receives blessing. It is good grace received and then given freely.

Passover is the anticipated endeavor to become the good grace and redemption this world desperately needs. If you celebrate the bread and wine, you join with God in what he is already doing in this world. Passover is about humanity becoming a partner with God in acts of restoration and reclamation.

If the goal for the bread and wine was only remembering, then promises of freedom and exodus would fall upon the deaf ears of a presently enslaved humanity. However, the divine purpose of the bread and wine finds its essence in the continual daily participation in the receiving and giving of good grace. When you eat the bread and drink the wine, you not only thank Jesus for his past sacrifice, but you, maybe even unknowingly, expect a present/future outpouring of his good grace. And that never disappoints.

Today when my family celebrates Passover, we gather with several other families, and we walk through the Passover story, and we are reminded, year after year, of how utterly amazing the love of Papa God is in our lives. We are reminded of our journey of freedom. We are reminded of how Papa pursued us, guided us with pillars of fire, opened the sea of self-doubt, and led us through to the Promised Land. We pour out our story of good grace because we know, beyond a shadow of doubt, that it will ignite your story.

Blades of Grass

When my kids were younger, they loved those sweet tart bones from the candy dispensers in Walmart. They're like SweeTarts, but they look like dog bones. They cost a quarter, and they do sell the exact same candy in the candy aisle, hermetically sealed, fresher, and at a lower unit price.

But I go for the dispensers every time. One day we were leaving Walmart, and we gave my young daughter a quarter. She dropped it in the slot. She turned the handle, and at the same time she opened the little door and all the candy poured out on the ground. She was devastated. I bent down to mourn with her when a quarter dropped to the ground and rolled a foot or so. I kid you not. A quarter dropped from the air and hit the ground. My wife and I both stared at it for a few seconds. I said, "Where did that come from?"

She looked at me and said, "I don't know."

My daughter got her candy. A great spiritual victory. I couldn't believe it. Utterly amazing. Let me tell you, I walked away from Walmart amazed at my God that he sent a quarter for sweet tart bones candy for my daughter. Yes!

Have you ever been a part of something like that? Maybe not a quarter materializing out of thin air for candy sweet tart bones, but some miraculous experience that left you in awe of the one who provides?

There's a story in 1 Kings 18 about a man named Elijah. He just won a great victory on Mount Carmel. Through Elijah, God defeated 450 prophets of Baal by sending fire from heaven to completely burn up the entire sacrifice even soaked in water. This was a great spiritual victory. Everyone knew that Yahweh was the most powerful God.

Can you imagine being part of something as extraordinary as that? Just being a part of the miraculous would leave you with a powerfully renewed spiritual confidence.

But you know what they say: the higher you go, the harder you crash. The author writes, "Jezebel sent a messenger to Elijah, saying, 'So may the gods do to me and more also, if I do not make your life as the life of one of them by this time tomorrow.' Then he was afraid, and he arose and ran for his life."[39] So here's Elijah calling down fire from heaven—a great spiritual victory. He's on top of the world. Yet a simple threat forces Elijah to crash. It took the wind out of his sails.

Isn't our journey of faith like that most of the time? We could be so excited and amazed one day, and maybe a week later, a day later, a minute later, something happens to us. We get news of something, and we crash. One day we could be walking in the Garden of Eden, and a few moments later we find ourselves walking in a desert.

After the threat, Elijah runs to Beersheba (it sits on the edge of the Negeb Desert), and the author writes that he went a day's journey into the desert. He traveled a day deeper into the dry wilderness. Now, it barely rains in the Negeb. The northern part of Negeb near Beersheba gets about eight to twelve inches of rain per year. The further south you go, the less it rains.

By the end of our story, Elijah ends up at Mount Horeb. It hasn't rained there in decades. It's a dry place, very fitting to where he is at spiritually. And maybe it's a place where you are now in your journey of faith. I'll be honest, it's a place where I have found myself living in the past.

I have always been taught that living in the desert is not a place where you want to be. It's a place of struggle; it's a place of intense heat; it's a place where you find little rest. And I have found myself living there a time or two in the past, and maybe you find yourself there as well.

Elijah is in the desert with no food or water, with no rest from the brutal sun and heat. He sits under a broom tree and cries out, "I have had enough, Lord."[40]

"I have had enough, Lord." Have you uttered those five words before?

I have said those words countless times during the affair, during the great sadness. Depression and discontentment covered my heart like frost covers the cold, hard ground. Yet there seems to be a yearning for the light of the sun to burn it off. But my heart erected a tent to keep off the rays of Jesus; it was called "Misplaced Identity." I began to think it was all about me. I chose to forget that Papa God adopted me into the kingdom of light.

> I will be a Father to you, and you will be my sons and daughters. (2 Corinthians 6:18)

> Yet to all who did receive him, to those who believed in his name, he gave the right to become children of God. (John 1:12–13)

> God sent his Son…to redeem those under the law, that we might receive adoption to sonship. (Galatians 4:4–5)

> The Spirit testifies with our spirits that we are God's children. (Romans 8:16)

> He predestined us for adoption to himself as sons though Jesus. (Ephesians 1:5)

Our adoption ushers in a divine identity that shapes the course of our destiny, yet there still requires a stewardship. Our adoption is final, but our acceptance is a choice. We must choose daily to walk as sons and daughters.

My "misplaced identity" ushered me down another aisle of life. I subconsciously believed I could do it on my own. This thing called life could be done successfully on my own; egotism and pride became me. Yet Papa God would continue searching, looking for his lost son. He never gives up looking; He never abandons the search. He is reckless in his pursuit. His desire is that we walk confidently and boldly as his children.

And when we fail to walk in our identity as sons and daughters of divine royalty, we may find ourselves lying face down under a broom tree. We may wake up to ourselves shouting, "I have had enough, Lord."

I think we all have said this in our lives at some point. God, I have had enough. I can't take this anymore. But I want to offer you some hope, or better yet, some grace and celebration. Bear with me; I promise this will all tie together in the end. I want to give you a little geography lesson with two points, and I want you to understand that what you are about to read is vital to understanding what happens in our lives.

Elijah found himself in the Negeb Desert. In the desert there is no water and no food, which is very bad news if you're a sheep. You're living in this place, and it's a struggle to eat and drink. Every day is a struggle to survive.

One of the biggest problems in this area is flash floods. It hardly ever rains in this area; and down south further, it rains once, maybe twice, a decade. But in the mountains, many miles away, it rains hard. There are flash floods that charge down the mountains, carving huge trenches as they run through.

These waters charging through the desert carves out huge canyons called wadis, and many shepherds die every year because of these flood waters. These waves of water, sometimes twelve to twenty feet high, will charge through these wadis, dragging stones and boulders the size of small cars. These flooded wadis were, and still are, a huge problem in that area.

Now in the bottom of these wadis, after the floods have receded, you'll find pools of water left behind, and sheep will wander down into the wadi looking for these pools of water.

But the sheep, not knowing when the floods are coming, will stay and drink. Suddenly, another flood will rip through the wadi and carry them away. But if the shepherd is with them, they're safe; they're safe because the shepherd knows when the floods come. The shepherds talk about these pools of water as "quiet waters," or "waters of peace."[41] These pools of water were safe as long as the shepherd was with you; these were peaceful waters if the shepherd led you there.

It's interesting, isn't it, that these waters in the wadis—so full of danger, distress, and chaos—can be called peaceful and quiet as long as the shepherd is with you? If the shepherd is with you, it's safe, it's right, it's good, it's going to be okay.

That was point one. Now point two. I want you to remember that this is the desert—no rain, no water—which results in no food. During the day, it is usually 100–120 degrees. It's so hot, it heats up the sand and the rocks. They say you can almost sizzle an egg on the rocks. Yet every day, late in the afternoon, a strong cool breeze begins blowing from the Mediterranean Sea.

As this cool, humid breeze blows in and meets the hot, sizzling rocks, enough moisture condenses and drips off the rocks and literally overnight, little patches of grass grow out from the rocks. Not large patches, more like a dozen blades of grass grow five to six inches overnight. And in the morning, the shepherd will lead those sheep to the rocks, move them around, exposing the blades of grass, and the sheep will have enough food for a mouthful. And the shepherd will move to the next one.

So shepherding becomes leading the sheep from one patch of grass to the next. And the Middle Easterner, to this day, calls this the "green meadows of the shepherd."[42] And the sheep aren't worried because they have a shepherd.

And if the grass is gone today, don't worry; we have a shepherd who will lead us there tomorrow one mouthful at a time.

There's a man named David, the shepherd king, who wrote much of what we call the Psalms. One in particular resonates with me:

> The LORD is my shepherd; I shall not want.
> He makes me lie down in green pastures.
> He leads me beside still waters.
> He restores my soul.[43]

I'll pause and let you soak that in for a minute.

All the sudden, Psalm 23 takes on a new meaning. Sometimes when we read the Bible, we create an American picture of a Middle Eastern idea. So we think of meadows as acres of lush grass or walking chest high in wheat, but that's not what's in the desert of Israel. This is not a land of plenty; this is a land of desert, a place of struggle. Yet God provides more than enough to make it.

Back to our story. Elijah is under a broom tree praying to die, crying out, "I have had enough." And an angel appears with…take a guess. No, not grass. Rather a cake baked on hot stones and a jar of water.[44]

Food and water, more than enough to make it. At a time when you find yourself in the desert and you cry out, "God, I have had enough," he gives you what you need to make it. He not only gives you what you need to quench your thirst, but the desert becomes a safe place, a peaceful place, a protected place in the midst of turmoil and chaos.

I have always been taught that the desert is not a place you want to be as a Christian. I disagree. The longer I'm walking with God, the more I'm realizing that the desert is the only place I want to be. It's there that Holy Spirit reveals himself in ways you can't possibly imagine. Because you have no other choice but to depend on him.

At a time in your life when the floodwaters come raging through, and the sun is so hot, he provides just enough to make it one day at a time. Think about a time in your own life when the heat of the sun in the desert was so intense that you thought to yourself, *I don't know if I can make it. I can't go on another day. Life in this desert is awful.*

Because we read Psalm 23, and I think, *God, where are the green pastures? Where is the overabundance? Where's the acres of abundance? This is what you promised me as your child. God, where are the still waters? You're my shepherd, and you're not leading me there. You're leaving me to suffer this intense heat and floods all by myself. God, I have had enough.*

Have you had similar thoughts?

But the beauty of this story of Elijah and Psalm 23 is God saying, "Life in the desert is good. I am the Good Shepherd. If you stick with me, you will not lack anything. We will make it. It's going to be okay. We're going to make it."

When I was going through my affair, my wife wrestled with God. Questions emerged: "Why is this happening? Where are you, God? When will it end?" She would cry out phrases like "I have not enough. I don't understand."

She would tell you now that although she was at a breaking point, she began to notice the blades of grass available every day.

She began to see the blades of grass and the pools of water after the floods: a group of godly friends who would not abandon her, who fought for us through prayer, tears, and fellowship.

The blades of grass took form in what she called "little bites of hope." God would give her scripture to breathe, prayers to pray, hopeful thoughts, conversations with random people who offered encouragement, song lyrics that lifted the depths of her soul. She began to see that through this life in the desert, God is shepherding us twelve blades of grass at a time.

It's as if God is saying, "I won't make your problems go away, but I will give you more than enough to make it. I will give you enough food to cease your hunger. I will give you enough water to quench your thirst. I will give you enough sleep to make it. I will provide enough finances to pay your bills. I will send someone else into your life to replace the one you lost. I will drop a quarter from the sky for sweet tart candy bones. I will give you a five-minute conversation with a senior pastor who has words of comfort and encouragement."

When your life seems miserable, and you're hurting, Papa God will give you twelve blades of grass, little bites of peace and hope. God will not make your problems go away, but he will give you whatever you need to handle it—more than enough. God has promised us "the green meadows of the shepherd" and "quiet waters" more than enough to deal with your life right here, right now, twelve blades of grass at a time. You're going to make it; it's going to be okay.

Shalom

I woke up at 5:30 a.m., stretched, and thought about rolling out of bed. Then I remembered where I was, and a great anticipation came over me. I popped out of bed, brushed my teeth, changed my clothes, and almost skipped down the stairs.

As I walked out the front doors of the hotel, I inhaled deeply. The crisp, cool air actually hurt my nose for a second, but, wow, did the Sea of Galilee smell good. It was January in Israel, and life was good.

An old man walked past me. I nodded at him; he responded with "Shabbat shalom."

Uh, yeah, "And to you, sir, a Shabbat shalom as well."

That phrase resonated within the depths of my soul. As I heard it and repeated it throughout the day, it caused my soul to leap in celebration. I asked our Jewish tour guide the significance of the phrase. I knew *Shabbat* meant Sabbath and *shalom* meant peace, so I assumed it meant "Peace to you on this Sabbath Day." But our guide painted the word picture of a deeper and more significant meaning: may you be restored to wholeness on the blessed Sabbath.

I'm sorry. Would you repeat that?

May you be restored to wholeness on the blessed Sabbath.

May you be restored to wholeness. Yes, please.

Let's explore this concept of shalom for a moment. It means far more than to be free of conflict. To ancient rabbis and people living in that day, shalom was a state of harmony. Shalom means to be utterly complete and whole, in harmony with God not just spiritually, but mentally, physically, emotionally, and soulfully.

Shalom is like your overall health and wellness being in harmony with God. It's your mind, body, soul, spirit…it's your whole person being in harmony with God. It's being made whole with life and body. It's your mind not racing with all the busyness and worries; it's the anxieties not being there; it's the calm from being at peace with God. Shalom is the whole harmony that comes from every dimension of your being in tune with the God who made you.

When my oldest daughter was four years old, she loved puzzles. I know what you're thinking, and yes, she is advanced. She would put together puzzles all day long. But being young and messy, the pieces of the puzzle would oftentimes become missing. And she was unable to leave the puzzle unfinished (that's her mom's side coming out). I would hear her calling for me from the other room, "Daddy, daddy, daddy, I can't find the last piece. Will you help me find the last piece?" And I would rush over and spend the next hour on my hands and knees searching for that last piece.

Shalom is as if your life is a puzzle, with the pieces being those of spiritual, mental, physical, emotional, social. And shalom means all of those pieces of your life fit together and are in place for a complete picture.

So Jesus, in essence, is coming into this world of chaos, confusion, anxiety, loss of identity, feelings of self-inadequacy, slavery. He's born into this world and in essence says, "I am here to put all of the pieces of your life back together again that every last piece is found and joined together to be in complete harmony with God, with me."

That's shalom. In fact, let's take this from another angle. In Exodus 4, we find the story of Moses being called by God to deliver his people from the Egyptians because God wants to set his people free. So Moses was living without conflict for forty years in the desert. He sees a burning bush, realizes his calling, and then talks it over with his father-in-law, Jethro. And this is the response Jethro gives: "Go in peace."[45]

Wait a minute. Moses is going back to the land of darkness, bondage, slavery, conflict, confrontation, turmoil, stress, confusion, frustration, and his father-in-law says to him, "Go in shalom"?

How often do you and I allow our experiences in life determine our relationship with God? How many times have we found ourselves in a land of darkness and confusion and begin to think that God is not around? Or we have found ourselves in a land of conflict and stress and begin to think that God is not speaking into our lives? Or found ourselves in a land of bondage and slavery and begin to think that God does not hear our cries? When in reality, God desires us to live with this awareness that in all situations, we can live in shalom.

So Moses is going into this land of negativity, slavery, and restlessness, and Jethro says, "Go in shalom." Go with all of the pieces of the puzzle in place. May you be restored to wholeness even there.

Remember my story of Makiah and her love for puzzles? When she couldn't find a piece of the puzzle to complete it, she would call out, "Daddy, daddy, daddy, will you help me find the last piece?" And when I did find it and hand it to her, she would place it where it needed to be, and the entire puzzle was whole and complete. She always looked up, smiled at me, and said, "Daddy, you saved me."

Daddy, you saved me. Yep, I suppose I did.

In the Middle Of

It's pretty sweet when you can walk into a room through a locked door. Did I mention the door never opens? You literally just pass through the door. And can you imagine being in the room when someone does that? You would be thinking there must be something pretty special about this person.

In John 20, Jesus has been resurrected and walks through the locked door to stand in the middle of his disciples and speak for the first time to them. And his very first words after his resurrection were, "Peace be to you."[46] Shalom be to you. Powerful words at a powerful time in human history. Jesus has been resurrected. Feel free to shout, "*Yes!*"

And the first time he sees his disciples he says, "Peace be with you." Now there is so much wrapped up in these four words. A complete lifestyle of restoration exists within these four words. Peace be with you.

The Greek word for peace is *eirene*. It means to experience harmony and rest with life around you. This is the closest word for shalom that the Greek has. *Eirene* is the overall quietness of your soul being at rest with relationships of people around you. It's being in harmony with God and his direction in your life. *Eirene* is allowing your soul the assurance of salvation, being at rest with God.

Peace in the English language means rest from something: rest from war, conflict, chaos, confusion. Because of that, we understand peace as an absence of something. But that's not biblical peace. Biblical peace is not the absence of something; it is the presence of Someone.[47]

And Jesus says, "Peace be with you." These are words that speak to us even today. Maybe you have a vision of self-inadequacy where you think you're never good enough—peace be with you. Maybe you have all kinds of baggage from a messed-up life beyond your control—peace be with you. Maybe your life is in chaos and confusion from past decisions that have wounded you deeply—peace be with you.

See, these are active living words. These are words that we can enter into. To fully understand what John is writing here, we need to dive into the cross for a brief moment.

In John 19, as Jesus hung on the cross, a few people stood near him: his mom, his aunt, another Mary, and another Mary (Magdalene), and a disciple.[48] I want to give you a couple of thoughts about this scenario. First, the phrase "standing nearby" in verse 26 is actually only one Greek word, *peristemi*, and it means "to stand nearby, in close proximity to, to bring into one's fellowship and intimacy." I mean, this is being very close to someone, being very near them.

Now what's interesting is that John only uses this word, *peristemi*, two times in his writing. And each time is in the story of the cross. The first is in the passage where the soldier punched Jesus in the face.[49] I mean, you're looking at a couple of feet between them. It was that close. That's *peristemi*. And that's what John wants you to see.

John has a purpose when he writes. The book of John is one of those books in the Bible that you can read at face value and receive spiritual influence. And at the same time, if you wish to go deeper, he has so many different layers throughout his writings. What I'm learning about John is that he chose each word very carefully. John gives you a chance to go deeper with each word he writes. So we get to a word like *peristemi*, and we can read it as just standing nearby, or we can read it as being so close to Jesus, most likely a couple of feet.

The second use is in John 19:25. This group of women and his disciple stood by Jesus. Not somewhere close, but they were *peristemi*; they were in Jesus's fellowship and intimacy. They were that close.

Sometimes we get the idea that Jesus was crucified high on a hill somewhere. And if you passed by, all you could see were silhouettes high on a hill. You have all seen the Sunday school paintings plastered over your church. Yet Jesus was not crucified on a hill but at the bottom of a hill. Read your Bibles carefully. It does not say he was crucified on a hill; it says he was taken to a hill and crucified there.

Roman law said that you had to crucify a person at eye level with those who walked by. They had to be at eye level to persuade you not to defy Roman law. You couldn't ignore them; they would be right in your face as you passed by.[50] And if you saw them, you knew that if you broke Roman law, this punishment was possible. It kept people on the straight and narrow. Jesus was right in your face as you walked by.

And here was the trifecta of Marys, his mother's sister, and John standing near the cross. Standing *peristemi* to Jesus. Standing so close that they would have Jesus's fellowship and intimacy. Or being so close, you could see his lungs breathe in and out; you could smell the sweat coating his body; you could hear the drops of blood as they hit the ground. That's *peristemi*.

Now let's get back to the disciples in the locked room. Gathered inside this small room were the twelve disciples, and Luke says there were more with them: the women, the three Marys, maybe more. All of them squeezed into a small room. That's the setting, very close to one another.

And Jesus came and stood among them. "Stood among them." When I first looked at these words, I wanted it desperately to be the word *peristemi*. How great would that have been? But he doesn't use that word here. It's different. Instead of using *peristemi*, he uses the words *istemi mesos*—stood in the middle of. Now what's fascinating is the idea of the comparison between these two phrases. Near the cross they were *peristemi* to Jesus.

See, *peristemi* is something that you and I would do with someone else. Jesus was hanging on the cross. He chose to be helpless. Jesus was standing before the official who punched him. He was helpless as much as a human could be. In other words, these people presented themselves to Jesus in his helpless state. *Peristemi*, the two times it's used in John, is related to Jesus choosing to be helpless and weak. John can't use this word in the resurrection story. He can't. Jesus is not helpless anymore. He has risen, and he comes to this room with the disciples, and he *istemi mesos*.

Istemi mesos means "to stand." To not only stand but to "stand firm, to stand immovable, to stand like a foundation who does not waiver." Jesus is the Rock, and he stood like that smack dab in the middle of those people. He stood like that in the middle of confusion, chaos, unbelief, feelings of self-inadequacy, fear.

The same intimate setting as the cross, but now he has been resurrected. He is immovable; he is unwavering. Jesus is the Rock, and he says, "Peace be with you." These are words of harmony and restoration. Peace be with you. Let those feelings of confusion, chaos, self-inadequacy, fear—let those feelings melt away when you hear my words, "Peace be with you." It's Jesus offering us harmony and restoration smack dab in the middle of our hectic, busy, demanding, confusing, muddy lives. Peace be with you. Restoration is found in hearing the very words of God. Shalom be with you.

Shalom comes with the presence of Jesus in our lives even in the midst of everything else.

Daddy, you saved me.

Now celebrate the restoration to wholeness.

Deer and Callings

I remember September of 1997 was warmer than usual. That sticks in my mind not because of the temperature, but because I had never tested God before that day. I went to my usual spot of thinking and praying: a hundred-acre camp in the boonies of Southern Ohio. I often went there to walk on the trails and see the wildlife. It seemed the trees and rolling hills went on forever. It's beauty unmatched.

In quiet places like that, God seemed to always be a bit louder than usual in my heart. But this time, I was feeling completely discouraged and frustrated. I was faced with a decision. I was self-employed as an independent contractor, installing windows and doors, making pretty good money. But I was never content. There was always a restlessness deep within my heart for being on the front lines within the kingdom of God, a longing to lead the most powerful force on the planet, the church.

But I never felt qualified or worthy enough to be used in such a profound way. As my early years went on, the feeling grew stronger until now, at its pinnacle, I was confronted with the possibility that, perhaps, I would not be content in life unless I became a pastor.

I remember thinking that God couldn't use me that way. I partied too much in college until I finally graduated eight and a half years later. I had no direction or purpose, and my life reflected that. But now, devoted to God, could he possibly be urging me to be a pastor? No way.

But as I walked and prayed, that feeling became a relentless pounding in my heart. I had to do it. But the battle in my mind was almost unbearable. I needed confirmation. I needed God to confirm the word he gave me deep in my soul. I needed something.

I climbed the familiar hill that hosted three white crosses. This spot was consistently valuable to me throughout my earlier years as God seemed to always show some revelation into his grace and love. And this time was no different; I needed a revelation. I longed for it. If this is what you want me to do, God, then show me something.

My knees hit the ground in desperation as I cried out, "I don't think I'm worthy enough. I'm not sure I'm the one. Show me, God. Show me something. If you want me to do this, I don't know, God, send a deer." What happened next would leave me in awe for the rest of my life. The biggest buck I had ever seen came charging through the ravine below me and up the other side as if God himself reached down and slapped its butt.

My mouth dropped open in awe as shalom came over me in a powerful way. This is it, I thought. This is my destiny. Yet God wasn't done yet. Two young fawns came out of the bushes to my right and began to run and play with each other, sometimes standing on their back hooves, batting each other, like a scene from the classic *Rudolph the Red-Nosed Reindeer*.

That scene was overwhelming to me as I watched them play. My feelings were uncontrollable as I wept and sobbed. They heard me and ran off, but my confirmation was given. My destiny was etched in stone. I was going to be a pastor and lead the church to great and powerful things. I left that camp with a new sense of purpose, a divine calling, excited to join God in bringing the kingdom of God everywhere.

Fast-forward thirteen years, I was sitting on my bed with a pistol in my hand as my feelings were once again out of control. The affair had ended, but the consequences were unbearable. Visions of those deer replayed over and over in my mind. God called me, and I spit in his face. I believed I would never be a pastor again. I screwed it up. It's over. My destiny was lost, at least I believed it at the time.

What do I do now? Nothing. My calling was negated, and I was lost. Hopelessness and oppression powerfully flowed over me that day. I pulled the bolt back on my pistol. I watched the bullet enter the chamber. I slowly put the gun to my head, my finger on the trigger. I again watched that big buck run through the ravine. "I'm sorry, God," I cried. "I gave it away. I'm useless. I'm nothing." I put the pistol in my mouth. Tears flowed.

I had always thought depression was an excuse to not be effective in life. But now, it slapped me, abused me, and molested me. I believed there was no way out, and here I was, with a gun in my mouth, my finger on the trigger, wondering if I could do it.

I remember thinking, *At their wedding, who would walk my girls down the aisle? I can't do this. There has to be another way. God, I have had enough.* I unchambered the round, took the clip out, and threw the pistol down on the bed. I was still shaking and crying so intensely that I couldn't see God there. But he was.

Years later, when I replayed that moment in my mind, I again broke down in tears. Not because it was too painful, but because it was then that I saw where God was at that moment. God was *istemi mesos*, standing in the middle of that chaos as a rock. Jesus was there offering me little bites of hope and grace, "It's going to be okay." Holy Spirit was drawing circles around me whispering, "There's something better around the corner. Hold on, son. It's not over yet."

It's there, in the silent darkness that the presence of Jesus thunders across your heart beckoning you to choose the expectation of the coming promise.

* * * * *

When you foster an attitude of daily celebration, you begin to develop a healthy expectation of God's coming promises. You rejoice with the promise of coming, not in the arrival. Celebration draws the infinite circles of God's promises around your life and gives you shalom as you wait for what's to come.

Imagine life as a mountain where your quest is to reach the summit, and not simply arrive but arrive with all of you there. In the book of Exodus, God tells Moses, "Come up to the mountain and wait there…then Moses went up the mountain…the glory of the Lord dwelt on Mount Sinai."[51] What's interesting is that the Hebrew words for "wait there" actually means to "be there." Yet to the early translators, that didn't make sense. "Come up to the mountain and be there." Why would God tell Moses to come up to the mountain and be there? Once Moses is on the top of the mountain, where else would he be? So they thought perhaps "wait there" would fit better.

Yet it doesn't. Maybe it's this idea when you climb your mountain of life expecting to reach the top, yet every day is a difficult climb. You expend all kinds of physical, emotional, and spiritual energy, oftentimes with very little results. "Will I ever get there? Where is the end? God, I have had enough." And when we reach the top of that mountain, whatever it may be, we check out. We reach the top, and we feel like we accomplished something, and we shut down.

Yet God says when you climb the mountain and reach the top, you had better be there—all of you, be there. Why? Because he's about to show up with all his glory. And if we are not all there, we will not see it.

Grace sets you to that quest, but celebration pushes you forward; it gives you that nudge you need to go over the top. Daily celebration allows you to reach the top of your mountain and be there.

Joy

One who did not see the joy of the water-drawing
celebrations, has not seen joy in his life.

—Talmud, Sukkah 51a–b, 53a

The Essence of Joy

I was floating on the Dead Sea one chilly afternoon. I found it utterly amazing that I could float without trying to float. The salt content is so high that it kept me from sinking. The experience was surreal.

The Dead Sea. Named for the fact that nothing can survive in the sea. Fish, aquatic life, and plants cannot survive due to the high salt content. The only thing that can survive there are tourists—floating tourists.

The sea is fed by one main river: the Jordan. Yet what makes it dead is the fact that nothing flows out of the sea. The salt cannot escape. Fresh water enters, but the salt immediately taints it. Water flows in, but nothing flows out, so we call that dead. It's interesting, isn't it? For the fresh water to be effective for life, there must be an exit flow.

While at the Dead Sea, my tour guide mentioned there was a fruit that only grows around the Dead Sea area. He called it the 'osher fruit. What's fascinating is that this fruit, the size of a peach or apple, grows on trees in little clumps of three or four. When you pick it off the tree, it feels like a juicy fruit, and it looks delicious. But if you bite into it, it pops open with a puff of dust. It's dead and empty on the inside. Because of the wrong water-to-salt balance, the fruit never fully develops. It looks delicious on the outside, but the inside is dead.

Or we could say, because living water simply entered the sea and never exited, the fruit never developed as it should. Hold that thought.

Joy is an essential aspect of Holy Spirit inspired life. In fact, joy is one of the fruits that one grows in their life when they are full of Holy Spirit. When the Spirit resides in you, joy grows into something delicious.

The Greek word is *chara*, and it implies an inner gladness or deep soaked pleasure. This type of deep *chara* does not flow from circumstance or present experience, but rather with the understanding of the presence and promise of Jesus. The Greek word for grace is *charis*, which finds its root word as *chara*. See, that deep-soaked pleasure, not as an outcome of any circumstance, but as a way of being, recognizes the gift of daily grace.

In other words, joy is the response of those who see God's grace at work daily. And because Jesus offers daily grace, we can claim it and respond with inner gladness despite what we are going through. That's why James can write,

> Count it all joy, my brothers, when you meet trials of various kinds.[52]

Why? Because Jesus said, "My grace is sufficient for you."[53]

There is a daily grace available to you in every situation, allowing you, if you take it, to bring a deep-seated joy in your life. And to not only experience it but share it with those around you. See, Holy Spirit desires joy to not only pool up inside you, but also to flow from you.

My voice of Waldorf and Statler loved to keep the Spirit's joy on the inside where it developed too high a salt content. It ended up killing life on the inside. They would say things to me like:

> You can't do that. People will think you're weird.
> Don't express it that way. People will think you're an idiot.
> Don't dance at this wedding. Pastors don't dance.

Essentially, the voice of Waldorf and Statler starved out the expression of joy in my life. It found its power in a false understanding of my identity. I didn't understand how Jesus saw me, nor did I understand his expectation of my acceptance of that truth.

See, joy is fully experienced when it flows out. When joy flows, the salt content balances, and delicious fruits emerge. When joy flows, the dead come alive. Joy is cultivated when you plant yourself by the right water.

Dance

Have you ever been so excited and joyful about something that you began dancing with no music playing, at least not audibly? But you find yourself shaking your groove thing to an inner rhythm. It's a divine encounter. And it is such a letdown when your husband or wife doesn't shake it with you.

The writers of 1 Chronicles and 2 Samuel tell a story of King David bringing the Ark of the Covenant into the city of Jerusalem. There is a sense of wonder, excitement, and passion as the ark makes its way down the street. His body is infused with energy, delight, and excitement—a bomb ready to explode with anticipation. When the ark lands itself in the temple, something will be different in Jerusalem. The presence of God will be here powerfully and abundantly. He cannot contain himself any longer, so he dances. Because sometimes that's the only natural expression for sheer joy.

Yet his wife Michal watched him from a window, and the Bible says, "She despised him with her heart."[54] The enemy of joy is not sadness, mourning, or grief; it's hate. You can be in mourning, sadness, and grief yet still experience the joy of the Lord. But you cannot hate, despise, and look down on someone through the eyes of joy. It just doesn't happen.

If you find yourself criticizing, disliking, despising, judging, looking down on someone else, you cannot call yourself a joyful person. It just can't happen.

Nonetheless, David dances out of sheer joy, delight, and anticipation that something will be different now. So the two writers record this excitement with four Hebrew words: *raqad, pazaz, karar,* and *sachaq*. Let's explore for just a moment.

Raqad means "to spring wildly for joy." It is also used in Joel 2[55] for the description of an approaching army moving so fast that they seem to *raqad* over the mountaintops.

Pazaz can be interpreted as "to leap as if separating the limbs." In other words, there is such an excitement within a person that jumping and leaping become so extreme that it looks as if their arms and legs will separate from their body.

Karar means "to whirl and twirl." Some scholars also paint a picture of the frolic and play of a lamb without a care in the world, wholly confident in the presence of the shepherd.[56]

Sachaq means "to take great pleasure in something," and it's also the word for laugh. *Sachaq* expresses a deep joy that comes with the promises of God, rejoicing in what's to come that the joy of the Lord has an outward expression. *Sachaq* grabs that promise and adds a joyous laughter, a deep-seated joy, and an anticipated excitement.

Do you have a mental image of what is happening here? If David rejoiced like this, and he is a man after God's own heart, is it possible that Jesus, our God, also rejoiced this way?

There is a passage in Proverbs 8 that talks about how the universe was created—Proverbs 8.22–31:

> The LORD brought me forth as the first of his works,
> before his deeds of old;
> I was formed long ages ago,
> at the very beginning, when the world came to be.
> When there were no watery depths, I was given birth,
> when there were no springs overflowing with water;
> before the mountains were settled in place,
> before the hills, I was given birth,
> before he made the world or its fields
> or any of the dust of the earth.
> I was there when he set the heavens in place,
> when he marked out the horizon on the face of the deep,
> when he established the clouds above
> and fixed securely the fountains of the deep,

> when he gave the sea its boundary
> so the waters would not overstep his command,
> and when he marked out the foundations of the earth.
>
> Then I was constantly at his side.
> I was filled with delight day after day,
> rejoicing always in his presence, rejoicing in his whole world
> and delighting in mankind.

There are actually two different interpretations of this passage. There are some people who believe that this is not Jesus, but rather it is the concept of wisdom, and wisdom helped God create all things. And there are those others, such as myself, who believe this is a look into the six days of creation and how Jesus was there all along.[57]

The Hebrew word for rejoicing in the above passage, especially verses 30–31, is *sachaq*. So we get a picture of Jesus rejoicing during those first six days. Taking great pleasure and delight in the act of creation those first six days. If so, could we read Proverbs 8 like this?

> Jesus was *raqad, pazaz, karar,* and *sachaq* (or dancing) for his creation.

If you're like me, you're probably asking the question, "Why would Jesus dance this way as he created the universe? Why?" Because he saw something that made him so excited. Even before the first star was created, he saw something that stirred his heart. Paul writes in Ephesians 1:4, "He chose us in him before the foundation of the world, that we should be holy and blameless before him." Could it be that before the lights came on, in the total and utter darkness, Jesus had an image of you in his heart? He chose us. If he chose us, that means what? He knew us.

Even before the first star was set in place, before the foundation of the world, God knew you. He knew how many hairs are on your head, or not for some of us. He knew what you would become; how many kids you have; what sports you play; that you flunked your sixth-grade math test; that when you laugh, you snort; what makes you happy and sad; what makes you laugh, angry, and excited. He knows your struggles; how I would let him down time and time again. He knew you, and he chose you before the foundation of the world. And that image of you caused him to dance with such delight that the entire universe was set in place. The thought of you did that.

Now, some of you might be having a hard time wrapping your arms around this idea that the entire universe was danced into existence for you. So let's get this down to our level. Let me throw out some great and simple things in life.

Because of an image of you in the heart of Jesus, there are trees, oceans, smiles from a newborn baby, and tacos. Because of an image of you in the heart of Jesus, there's falling in love, laughing so hard your face hurts, a hot shower, rain, the beach, having your beautiful daughter fall asleep in your arms.

Running through sprinklers. Friends. Your first kiss. Watching the expression on someone's face as they open a much-desired present from you. Sunrise. Sunsets. Lying on your back watching the clouds. Music. Family. Rainbows. The Rocky Mountains. Swedish fish.

All things were created through Jesus because he danced with delight at what he saw, and he saw you. And what you see all around you is the evidence of an immense love that God has for you. His love is so great that it led him to the cross. The joy that comes from the thought of you set him to the cross: "who for the joy that was set before him endured the cross" (Hebrews 12:2).

You are the joy that was set before him. He looked down through the ages and saw you. He didn't see everything you're not, but he saw you. He saw you living out your first best destiny, and that ? him to the cross.

Jesus loves you exactly as you are but loves you too much to let you stay there. His desire is that every day you take one step closer to becoming the person he has intended you to be, and all of creation echoes that truth. It's Jesus saying, "I delight in you, and it's all for you. It's all for you."

Now, of course, we can say that it is all for his glory, but let's not diminish our standing in doing so. We cannot rob God's glory; none of us are that big. If we think we can steal God's glory away from him, then we have an ego problem.

> The heavens declare the glory of God. (Psalm 19:1)

> For from him and through him and to him are all things. To him be glory forever. (Romans 11:36)

> Everyone who is called by my name, whom I created for my glory, whom I formed and made. (Isaiah 43:7)

> But we all, with unveiled face beholding as in a mirror the glory of the Lord, are transformed into the same image from glory to glory. (2 Corinthians 3:18, NASB)

Although all creation shouts his glory, he is taking created humanity from glory to glory. It's important to know the starting point: glory. When you experience the good news of Jesus and surrender your life to him, you begin at glory.

Glory is the beginning, the foundation to build on. You are at glory. All creation shows his glory for us. In other words, we could say it like this: All creation testifies to his glory, of which we are a reflection. We are the reflection of the glory of God. Right now, as you are today, you are God's glory.

And the whole idea of creation is God giving us visual truth that he created us with value, worth, love, and acceptance. There is an ideal you that is in the mind of God, and so our invitation is that we live to be the people that God destined us to be: a reflection of his glory.

And the story since Genesis is that we, as human beings, find ourselves recreating our identity in other things, and that pulls us off course. And the story of the Bible is God persuading his people, "Hey, I created you with a purpose, with worth and value. Trust me. Just trust me."

Are you living in any way that disagrees with how God created you to be? God created you with value, significance, worth, importance, meaning, and for a purpose. And living outside of that truth is living a life that goes far below God's original design for you.

So the essence of creation is God saying, "I delight in you. It's all for you. My glory." It's all for you.

Living Water

I'm sure you found out by now that I love to ask why and how questions. I believe that the great and hidden things of Jeremiah 33:3[58] can only be obtained by asking questions of God. And so I ask. I ask a lot of questions.

As I walked into the Church of the Holy Sepulcher in Israel, I was immediately confronted with a hundred questions. It wasn't exactly how I imagined it to be. This was supposedly where Jesus died and was buried, but it became very iconic. Rather than pointing to Jesus, it seemed to be pointing to the icons, the symbols of the cross and tomb. In fact our guide had said that the Catholic Church had built a new improved tomb, capable of allowing a greater number of tourists through more quickly. And God said it was good…

However, our guide took us to a small cave etched into the stone face, just big enough for a person to crouch inside. Once we entered the small cave, about five yards inside there was three other small slots carved out of the rock. Two of them were walled up, but one was empty. I realized immediately that we were standing in a tomb. Our guide said this was the resurrection tomb. The empty one was Jesus's tomb. It may or may not have been the place, but there was something powerful about that site. Holy Spirit came over our small group powerfully.

As we exited the small entrance, I realized that it wouldn't have taken an enormous stone to cover the entrance. In fact, a few people could have moved the stone that would have guarded the entrance to Jesus tomb. So I started asking questions, and I found some answers that shaped my life.

In Mark 16, the author writes of the resurrection of Jesus. Jesus had died, and three women were on their way to the tomb to anoint Jesus's body with spices. As they were walking, they began asking the question, "Who will roll away the stone for us from the entrance of the tomb?"[59]

Just a thought: As large as the opening was to that tomb in the church in Israel, three women could have easily rolled away the small stone from the entrance. The question wasn't, "Who is strong enough to roll away the stone, because we certainly aren't." The question was about authority. When Jesus was laid in the tomb, and the stone rolled in front of it, the Bible said, it was sealed with Pilate's personal seal.[60] Breaking that seal would result in death. The "large" stone would have appeared "large" not because of size, but because of authority.

When the women asked the question, it was not about strength, but about authority. In other words, we could understand their question as "Who will move the stone, break the seal, and condemn herself to death? Which one of us will be the one?" Because, after all, humanity is subject to the earthly authority of their day. But Jesus isn't. So an angel moved the stone and sat on it.[61] That always makes me laugh. Jesus is far above all authorities, dominions, and powers.[62]

So let's ask a different question: Why was the stone rolled away from the tomb? Now, for some of you, the question may seem irrelevant. It's just a small detail in the great scheme of things, so why concentrate on something so small?

But I want to suggest that the stone being rolled away has a much deeper meaning for the world today. It answers the question for people who are struggling with what it means to be human. That sometimes—actually, most of the time—life isn't quite as easy as we make it out to be. Christians fall into this trap of saying, "Since I am a Christian, the world can't know that I struggle. I need to have the appearance that everything is all right." And it's not.

Mark 16 becomes more than a story of the struggle for three women going to a tomb; it becomes our journey of struggle and pain. I want you to enter into this story, and realize that their story is our story. Why was the stone rolled away from the tomb? In order for this question to make sense, we have to explore a certain description for Jesus.

The prophet Isaiah describes the coming messiah as a king who will reign in righteousness, a shelter from the storm, and streams of water in a dry place.[63] Streams of water in a dry place. How sweet is that?

The Hebrew word for dry place is *tsiyown*. It means "a dry place, a desert, a place free of any type of moisture and water." It's a place of struggle, pain, and despair. How many of you have found yourself in a *tsiyown*?

All of us, at one time or another, have found ourselves on a journey through a *tsiyown*. Maybe for you, a *tsiyown* is having an important decision to make about your life and finding out that you do not have a clear direction, and it's frustrating. You're walking through a *tsiyown*.

Maybe it's a relationship that you have that really matters to you, but there's this barrier between you both, and it seems that every time you get a little closer, the barrier thickens. And it's destroying what hope and love there could be in that relationship, and it's breaking your heart.

Maybe a *tsiyown* for you is an addiction that breaks your spirits every single day. And every time you seem to have a foothold, it beats you down until hopelessness and despair become a regular thing.

All of us have spent some time on a journey through the desert or a journey through despair, sadness, need, frustration, confusion, and pain. All of us have spent time on a journey through a *tsiyown*, and this description of Jesus as streams of water in a dry place is amazingly refreshing. It's Jesus getting at the core of what it means to be human. At the core of every human being lies this reality that throughout our lives, we will find ourselves on a journey through a dry place, and Christians are no exception.

So we begin to understand that there's so much wrapped up in this description of streams of water in a dry place. Maybe we could translate it as "he is our hope in times of despair. He is our answer in times of need. He is our joy in times of unhappiness."

Could it be that streams of water equals streams of joy and strength? Hold that thought.

One thing I love to do when I study is to find the first time something is mentioned in the Bible. So in Mark 16, when the stone is rolled away from the tomb, I went through Scripture and found the very first time in the Bible that a stone of some kind had been rolled away from something.

There's a story in Genesis 29[64] about Jacob finding a well with flocks of sheep waiting to be watered, but the stone was large and needed several shepherds to move it. After a quick reading, we could come to the conclusion that this is simply a story of Jacob coming across some shepherds who are about to water their sheep. But sitting it side by side with the Resurrection story, we find some amazing similarities.

Oftentimes, we picture wells in the ground that you would throw a coin into to get your wish. But sometimes wells, especially in the Middle East, were actually caves. And in these caves were springs of water, and the shepherds would roll a large stone in front of the opening of the cave to block any unwanted animals from taking the water.

The author writes in verses 3 and 8, "When all the flocks were gathered there, the shepherds would roll the stone from the mouth of the well and water the sheep," and "But they said, 'We cannot until all the flocks are gathered together and the stone is rolled from the mouth of the well; then we water the sheep.'"

It wasn't until the shepherds rolled away the rock that the sheep would have their thirst quenched. As the sheep journey through a *tsiyown*, their thirst and despair grow, and it isn't until the shepherds roll the stone away that the sheep are given an opportunity to have their thirst quenched.

The stone being rolled away gives the sheep the freedom and the ability to drink. If the stone is not rolled away, the sheep are restricted and bound to that thirst. The thirst is not quenched until the stone is rolled away.

Again, let's ask the question of the Resurrection story: Why was the stone rolled away from the tomb? The stone was rolled away, not to let Jesus out of the tomb. There is no stone in the universe that could hold Jesus. Jesus could have walked out of that tomb without even touching the stone. So the stone was not rolled away to allow Jesus to leave, but rather to allow us to see in. It was rolled away for us to have the outpouring of hope. It was rolled away for us to drink in that living water. It was rolled away to give us the freedom and ability to drink in the truth of who Jesus is and the hope of being delivered from despair.

It's more than just an empty tomb. It's the story of us emptying our despair and holding on to hope, answers, satisfaction, and joy as it flows from the tomb. It's a story of Jesus, the streams of living water, satisfying our deepest needs. It's a story of Jesus quenching our great thirst for happiness, joy, delight, and hope when we journey and live in a dry land of despair. It's Jesus saying, "I am with you now. Drink and be satisfied."

Joy flows powerfully to you. Open your hearts and drink it in.

A Good Bottle of Wine

I have some good friends that make their own wine. I'm not talking about a few bottles here and there, but three hundred to four hundred bottles at a time. And it's the best wine you'll ever taste. They often give me a few bottles to try their new batch. I love being the guinea pig.

I have found that I love the wine made with Chilean grapes. There's something different about the grapes in that area of the world. When they give me a few bottles, if it says anything Chilean on it, I save those bottles for special occasions. In fact, I'm positive that in John 2, Jesus turned water into a Chilean Cab. And I'm convinced that when Jesus returns and ushers his people into the great banquet, there will be tons of food, and the wine that Jesus serves will be my friends' wine uncorked and ready to be enjoyed.

I do love a good bottle of wine. I know some of you may gasp at that statement. Perhaps even question how a Jesus follower could even drink wine in the first place. But rather than justifying myself, I'll just leave you to wonder.

Wine. Certainly a fermented drink in biblical times; however, there is a deep symbolic use of this beverage throughout Scripture. Oftentimes throughout the Old Testament, when an author wanted to declare the idea of wrath, judgment, abundance, blessing, gladness, and joy, they would use wine as the picture.[65]

> Honor the LORD with your wealth and with the firstfruits of all your produce…and your vats will be bursting with wine. (Proverbs 3:9–10; here wine is symbolized as favor and blessing)

> Come, eat of my bread and drink of the wine I have mixed. Leave your simple ways, and live, and walk in the way of insight. (Proverbs 9:5–6; bread and wine is the way of insight and the Eucharist, or better yet, the good grace of Jesus)

> On this mountain the LORD of hosts will make for all peoples, a feast of rich food, a feast of well-aged wine, of rich food full of marrow,

of aged wine well refined. (Isaiah 25:6; this is a prophecy into the coming of Messiah, Jesus)

The point is, whether portrayed as wrath, judgment, blessing, or joy, wine is often connected to the presence of God. When the prophets and writers wanted the people of their day to understand the truth of God's presence, they painted word pictures of wine.

In the book of John, the author writes of Jesus's first miracle. He and his disciples were invited to a wedding. Long into the night, the bride and groom found themselves without wine for the rest of the party, which would have been a social disgrace. Jesus sensed the urgency of this situation and transformed water into wine.[66]

What's fascinating is at the time of this miracle, there was a cult that worshipped the Greek god of wine, Dionysus.[67] The practices of the Dionysus cult were most evident in its elaborate festivals. Often, these festivals became well known for their wild and passionate dancing in connection with the overabundance of wine. The purpose of becoming drunk with wine was to have Dionysus enter the body of the worshipper and fill him with energy and zeal, the spirit of the god. A popular story attributed to Dionysus was that on the sixth day of attending his annual feast, he transformed three sealed cauldrons of water into wine.[68]

Worldly joy is a counterfeit joy. Worldly joy comes from circumstances that cause a reaction within your life: as long as A happens to me, then B is the outcome. Joy becomes reactionary.

What happens when your mind is in a state of depression, even slightly? You are viewing the world through a blackened lens where nothing seems remotely good. The deeper your depression, the darker the lens until ultimately you can't find a silver lining on a silver cloud. Worldly joy is a reaction to worldly circumstances.

Yet biblical joy stems from a presence.

> For you make him most blessed forever; you make him glad with the joy of your presence. (Psalm 21:6)

> You make known to me the path of life; in your presence there is fullness of joy; at your right hand are pleasures forever. (Psalm 16:11)

he presence of Jesus delivers an expectant joy, regardless of circumstances, situations, and trials. Joy is the inevitable outcome of being in intimate connection with Papa God. Supernatural joy comes from God's presence, never from worldly pleasures.

The story of Jesus's first miracle, water into wine, is more than announcing his arrival onto the scene; it's a reclamation of the source of divine joy. The Dionysian cult required the consumption of too much wine. You must become drunk in order to experience the joy that Dionysus offered, and drunkenness always leads to a life less than what it could be. Yet Jesus shows up at a wedding and transforms water into wine; six stone jugs to be exact. Isn't that fascinating? Dionysus transformed three, yet Jesus transformed six. Jesus shows up and doubles the miracle of Dionysus in order that he may restore the celebration of godly joy. Jesus reclaimed the truth that he alone is the source of joy. We could also say that Jesus alone is the double portion of joy.

If you strive for joy from the world, you will always end up disappointed. It is temporary, weak, and tedious. It requires too much from you to sustain any lasting impression. It requires you to do. Yet resting in the joy of Jesus requires you to simply be. When you become a child of God, an inheritor of the kingdom of God as a coheir with Jesus, your standing allows you the benefit of divine joy. It's your standing that allows you the inheritance of joy. You simply be.

Worldly joy lasts only so long. It actually seems good until the miracle happens and the better stuff is served.

Gratitude

I just love celebrating Christmas. I like getting presents, but I love giving presents. And I love watching my kids open presents that I get them, and they sense the excitement and energy from Elisha and me right around October. We begin asking them what they want, and we have them circle stuff in the toy catalogs, and they end up circling every last thing. And then my wife and I begin to hype it up because you can never be too excited, right?

But when my oldest was two years old, Elisha and I hyped it up too quickly and with too much intensity. We found this out when she opened her night-before-Christmas present. We have this great tradition that every night before Christmas, we open one present, and that present is always new pajamas. Always PJs. Always. You never turn from this, neither to the right nor left. It is always PJs.

Two-year-old Makiah opened her night-before-Christmas present and stared at it with her head down. Finally, we said very excitedly, "Makiah, new PJs!"

She looked up at us with tears streaming down her face, weeping. Not even able to talk. Her face said it all: "This sucks." Or better yet, "It's the night before Christmas, and all I got was this lousy T-shirt."

Oops, my bad.

I'm sure we all have those types of people in our lives that can't seem to find a spirit of thankfulness in anything. They could have mountains of bills that they are having a hard time paying, and then one day receive a hundred dollars on their doorsteps, and they sarcastically respond, "Great. I have to pay bills with this."

We all have those people in our lives. Ones that can't seem to find a silver lining on a silver cloud. But don't we get like that sometimes when our spirit of thankfulness and gratefulness is buried under a ton of selfishness?

Another thing all my kids did was that they would open a present, briefly look at it, and immediately reach for another; never pausing, just looking forward to the next great thing. As a dad, my heart sank. I got you the exact thing you wanted, in the exact color. We spent weeks looking and trying to find it. And the closer we got to Christmas, the more we paid for it. Kids, how about a high five or a fist bump or something to show your gratitude? My heart sank a little.

I often wonder if that is the same with God. He created us in his image; we are created in the image of God. Doesn't that send shivers up your spine? Created in the image of the God of the universe. But through time, humanity has screwed it up, so our journey of faith is our journey to restore that image. It's our journey of restoration.

So God has given us good things along our journey to bring us back to him. But as a culture, we are moving so fast that sometimes we miss it. And our gratitude and thankfulness take a back seat. How can we become people who show a genuine and authentic gratitude with everything in life?

Paul writes a fascinating verse in Colossians:

> And let the peace of Christ rule in your hearts, to which indeed you were called in one body. And be thankful. Let the word of Christ dwell in you richly, teaching and admonishing one another in all wisdom, singing psalms and hymns and spir-

itual songs, with thankfulness in your hearts to God. And whatever you do, in word or deed, do everything in the name of the Lord Jesus, giving thanks to God the Father through him.[69]

This is one of those verses that is loaded with tension—peace of Christ. The Greek word for "peace" is *eirene*. It means to experience a harmony, security, and prosperity within the world. It means to experience the way of salvation. In other words, it is the tranquil state of the soul. A person of gratefulness allows their lives to be in complete harmony with God.

Then Paul writes, "And be thankful." I had always read this as a PS. But I think it's a bit different than that: Be thankful for his peace. Be thankful for the chance to be in harmony with God. Be thankful for the way of salvation.

He continues with the next phrase, which in the Greek should read, "Let the word of Christ dwell in you richly in all wisdom; teaching and admonishing one another in psalms, hymns and spiritual songs with grace singing in your hearts to the Lord."

A couple thoughts I would like to give you. First, the phrase "Let the word of Christ" is found only twice in the entire New Testament. Scholars believe it is the message that Jesus spoke and lived out during his ministry. What was the message of Christ? Again it is restoration, the good news, good grace. It's Jesus restoring us to an intimate relationship with God. It's Jesus restoring us emotionally, spiritually, mentally, physically, socially so we are able to enjoy a powerful relationship with God and with others. It's the ultimate power being made available to us to bring the life of heaven to earth. So Paul says let that message dwell in your hearts. It should take up permanent residence in you. In other words, it should be smack dab in the middle of everything you say and do. And when you do that, God's grace begins to sing in your heart with a tune that will set you to dance.

As grace sings its beautiful tune in your heart, you can't help but to be thankful about life, both good and bad. It's a tune that brings gratitude to God for just being alive. Because whatever you do, whether in word or deed, in everything give thanks to God.

The next phrase Paul writes is "in whatever you do," which means in "everything you do." Everything. From the most important all the way down to the most mundane, ordinary things you do. In everything, give thanks. Everything, whether good or bad. Everything. Give thanks.

Last Christmas was unbelievable. All three of my kids were the complete opposite from the early years. During the younger years, they cried and wept, always looking for the next best thing. Last Christmas, they opened every present as if it was the very first they had ever opened—they even cheered when they received new socks. And then they had the best excited faces. So beautiful. It didn't matter if it was the toy they longed for or a pair of underwear, they were genuinely excited and thankful for every last thing they got.

And as a dad, they made my heart smile. I wish I had gotten them more things just to see their faces when they opened them. I wonder if it's the same with God?

What things have you forgotten to say thank you for? What things in life have you missed because you're going so fast? In what areas of your life have you neglected God and his gifts? What things do you need to act as if it was the first time you experienced it—with wonder, excitement, and thankfulness?

Answers or Responses

Every epic adventure begins when one leaves home and enters a world of unknown danger and possibilities. This is the atmosphere that the would-be hero is thrust into. Without the atmosphere of danger, risk, and possibility, the story would be dead. You wouldn't pay $12.50 to watch Frodo Baggins bury the ring in his backyard and go back to reading under a tree. The adventure is in the leaving.

The same is true spiritually. So often, we stay at home with our doctrines and beliefs; we like to stay where it's comfortable, and we never step out into the unknown. We must begin to ask questions that are too big for us to answer on our own. Jeremiah 33:3 says, "Call to me and I will answer you, and I will tell you great and hidden things that you have not known."

Casual questions bring casual revelation. What we need is a deep burning that ignites the fury of abandonment. We must give up not the past spiritual truths that so many have sacrificed their lives for, but rather abandon the fear of the unknown.

Last year was the five hundredth year of the Reformation, an era when Martin Luther stepped out into the unknown with a million questions, challenging the very status quo of the religious institution. He shaped the course of history not by simply nodding yes in favor of tradition, but through humility, understanding the possibilities that came through God-sized questions.

Our lives are in need of a reformation, a new understanding of our divine identity. Unless we step out into the unknown with new questions, I fear we will be destined to repeat and/or continue to stay comfortable with understanding that simply warms the heart. God desires us to respond, "Did not our hearts burn within us?"[70] We must disrupt the ordinary ego of everyday thought. Deep God-inspired questions allow the mind to begin the process of leaving home. They set your heart to a new song.

New is in the heart of God: "Behold, the former things have come to pass, and new things I now declare; before they spring forth I tell you of them. Sing to the Lord a new song."[71] When we begin a life with Jesus, we become new creations with new power for new purposes. Jesus never intended for his new creations to continue doing the same things they have always done.

The right questions foster a newness. That's why we hear from children so many why questions. I tried my hardest to respond to every why question my kids had for two reasons: one, I wanted them to grow up understanding that questions were necessary in order to grow deep; and two, I wanted them to think that their dad was the smartest man on the planet. I suppose one out of two isn't bad.

This is why, in the rabbinic tradition, questions are essential. I have seen a conversation between two modern rabbis that consisted of only questions. If you could respond to a question with a question, then the dialogue would continue. Once an answer was given, the dialogue is over.

Answers end the conversation; responses continue the dialogue.[72] That's why so often through the Gospels, Jesus responds to a question with a question. It's the amazing art of rabbinic response, and it represents a great truth: questions are necessary.

We must begin to ask the questions that are shaking the foundation of our souls. The moment one stops asking questions is the moment complacency rears its ugly head. If questions cease, then mystery, wonder, and awe dissolve.

If I can explain everything within my Christian life and theology, if I can tell you exactly what everything means, then I have reduced God to what I know. There must be some mystery in my journey of faith. Mystery is just as important as revelation.

Our Western culture places knowledge over faith; or better yet, revelation over mystery. However, the Jewish culture places mystery over revelation. Western culture says you need to have all the answers, and then they need to be well documented. They need to be in list form, so it makes sense. Jewish culture says there is importance in the mystery, so Jewish culture loves questions that result with no answers.

In the Jewish culture there is no God-box. It took me a few decades to realize that it was okay to take God out of the evangelical box. In my pastoral years, I felt as if I needed all the answers. If I uttered the phrase, "I don't know," I felt as if I lacked wisdom, knowledge, and intelligence. I had to have an answer. For me, and perhaps for you, answers fueled ego.

How I needed mystery. In some unexplainable way, mystery unpacks divine humility and stamps it in your life. "Having no idea" unleashes Holy Spirit's power of wisdom and creativity. Oftentimes, out of my questions from desperation, I receive Holy Spirit's deepest responses. As long as you continue to think and ask, growth is happening.

Did you know there is no word in Hebrew for heresy? Heresy is simply wrong religious thinking. There is no word for wrong religious thinking in the Hebrew language; there is only wrongdoing. Why? Because we must remove God from the box we placed him in and begin to realize that he is much bigger than we could possibly comprehend, and profound questions that challenge the status quo are only the beginning of revelation.

Joy celebrates with the understanding that God, Jesus, and Holy Spirit are full of unknown mystery. Yet joy sets you on the adventure to discover the things your heart and soul long for.

Life

In the first-century world, *chayei* represented the quality within a human life that distinguished life from death. In other words, if you had *chayei*, you were breathing, and your heart was beating. You would be considered alive; you would have life within.

If you breathed your last breath, if you're heart stopped beating, it would have been said that you lost *chayei*. Humanity was built around the understanding that *chayei* was the essence, most significant vital element of human existence. Obviously, or you'd be dead.

Yet in the ancient world, everything was spiritual. So the question emerged: Are you really alive? You may be breathing; your heart may be beating; you may be going to work, watching TV, playing with your kids, driving your car, drinking coffee, going to church, shopping for Christmas presents, eating those salt and pepper pistachios that you love so much, but are you really alive? Or is there a sense of just going through the motions?

So *chayei* developed overtime to represent the very essence of contentment and celebration. If you enjoyed life, if you celebrated life, if you woke up in the morning with the uncontrollable awareness of gratefulness for that last breath you just took, then it would have been said that you had *chayei*. And if you didn't, then you were considered dead.

So let me ask again, are you really alive? Because *chayei* demands there be a continual expectancy to be daily revived, refreshed, and restored. Because deep within the essence of *chayei* lies the longing for grace upon grace. Because *chayei* says that life is to be enjoyed, celebrated, and relished.

This is Jesus's understanding of *chayei*. In the Greek New Testament, the writers used *zoe*, as the Greek understanding of the Hebrew word. Jesus said, "The thief comes only to steal and kill and destroy. I came that they may have *chayei* and have it abundantly." Or if you believe your life is monotonous, ordinary, unexciting, mundane, or common, perhaps someone has stolen, killed, and destroyed your God-endowed *chayei*.

Yet Jesus has come to give you *chayei* abundantly, to give you and me a life better than we could ever dream of. Your life's dream not of material possessions, money, or happiness, but rather a life of grace, celebration, joy, and contentment.

I struggle deeply with the overwhelming sense that perhaps we, as a culture, have lost our *chayei*, and we must reclaim it. We are in need to be daily revived, refreshed, and restored with grace upon grace. Because *chayei* says there was something better that you were before…

…before life happened, before decisions were made.

…before the ugliness and stench of selfishness entered the scene.

…before the foundation of the world.

And *chayei* suggests that you, once again, can return. *Chayei* says it's not over yet. Hold on, something better is, in fact, right around the corner. And in this process of restoration—of reclaiming your *chayei*—may you become as naked as I. Because at that moment, only in that moment, will you begin to dress yourself with the vision of what could be.

Afterword

When my first daughter was born, she came into the world with an attitude. And she decided that for the first two years, she would not sleep a night through. That was her decision, and she stuck to it. I could only imagine, at the time, that it was her repayment for removing her from the warm womb and thrusting her into a cold dark world. So she decided not to sleep.

After two years, we were exhausted, up every night multiple times. We were tired, frustrated, and on edge, so we decided to have another baby. Jim Gaffigan explains having his second kid like this: "Imagine you're drowning, and then someone hands you a baby." That's about right.

My second daughter came into the world smiling with not a care in the world. Makiah actually began to sleep the night through when Eden came into the world. Yet Eden wouldn't sleep for the next two years.

I remember it was a Thursday morning about 3:00 a.m., my lovely, wonderful, amazing daughter Eden was once again crying, and she would not stop. Elisha was getting frustrated; I was getting frustrated. Elisha had been up quite a bit longer than I had been, so I offered to take Eden downstairs to rock her and watch a little ESPN while I waited for her to stop crying.

I turned on the TV, which was the only light that was on downstairs. Eden was crying; I was frustrated. Have you ever been at a spot in your life where something was frustrating you, and those feelings make you want to pull your hair out, literally? Where is God?

I was almost there when I saw it. I saw it. I just happened to look up at the TV when I thought I saw something fly across the screen. Immediately, it had my attention. Then you start having that conversation with yourself: "Did I really see something fly across the screen, or am I so frustrated that I saw something that wasn't there?"

There was a commercial on TV during that time in life. It was the Orkin Commercial, the bug spray commercial, where they would show spiders and centipedes run across the TV screen to wake you up to buy their spray. I thought it was that for a brief moment.

Then I saw a flash again. It was black. If it was real, what was it? A bird? A butterfly? An evil spirit that left my daughter? I was opting for the last choice because she had actually stopped crying.

Then I saw it again. It was black and flying circles throughout the living room. A bat. We had a bat in our house. It was a rather large bat, and I was a little uncomfortable with that. So I cradled Eden close and ducked as I walked quickly upstairs.

I dropped off Eden with my wife about 3:45 a.m. and told her about the creature. She said, "You know, I thought I saw something fly around in here." Uh…So I walked downstairs and armed myself with the weapon that every husband uses for bats—the shotgun. No, I didn't; I grabbed the broom, and I waited for the creature to rear its ugly head.

I took two swings at it and missed it both times. I watched it fly off into the family room, and I waited for about thirty seconds. It did not come back. The stairs, I thought. Oh no, it's eating the face off of Makiah. That means she will be awake too. I ran upstairs.

I checked her room; not there. I closed the door and checked my bedroom; it was not there. I closed the door and went back downstairs. I explored the family room; it was not there. I tore apart the kitchen; it was not there. I went to the dining room; it was not there. I searched and hunted, explored and investigated from 4:00 to 6:00 a.m. I could not find the creature. I looked in every nook and cranny in our house. I found a lot of interesting things that were lost, but I did not find the bat.

I never did see the bat nor any evidence of a bat again. Anyway, I went back upstairs and told my wife another plan. I'm going to shut off all the lights downstairs and wait for the creature to return. Then it will die.

I headed off downstairs and sat on the rocking chair with my broom weapon—just waiting. As I sat there, I began to think about how just a couple of hours ago, I was feeling frustrated to the point of being very angry at Eden, pulling my hair out asking the question, "Where is God?" And now, I wanted to do nothing else but protect my family.

My question is this: Was it the bat that changed how I looked at life at 6:00 a.m. Thursday morning, or was it the awareness of something spiritual in the material world? Was it just a bat, or was it me waking up to a God who was right here and right now? In the dead center of intense feelings of frustration, anger, chaos, and confusion, there was God's presence waking me up to a new reality.

How many times have I been so caught up in the moment of life that I miss what God has for me? How many of us are wrestling with feelings, thoughts, and circumstances that we miss the significance of God in everything around us?

What have we missed? You know there won't be any tears in heaven, but I bet that might take a while. When we get there and look back on what we missed in everyday living, how we were so busy, and we look back and see what God had for us, but we missed it—I don't know, I think we'll shed some tears.

There is a new reality within this one where even through the heckles; jeers; despair; pain; misery; grief; lack of hope; hate; jealousy; anger; feelings of being unwanted, unloved, and unaccepted, Holy Spirit's voice is beckoning you; calling to you; whispering your divine identity, acceptance, and destiny into your soul. You must wake up to the new reality that right here and right now is the time. Your divine appointment is at hand.

In February of 2018, I attended a prophetic conference at Bethel Church in Cleveland. During the first morning there, I found a seat in the front row about thirty minutes before it kicked off. At these events, the front row is where the action happens.

A ministry team member sat beside me. We were making small talk about the weather, life, and jobs. She stopped me in midsentence and said, "God wants you to know that the situation in which your son was born into has been completely redeemed."

Rewind eight years. In May of 2010, Elisha showed me a white stick with two lines on it. She was pregnant. I was done with kids after my second was born. Two daughters seemed to be enough for me. So when Elisha presented me with the white stick, it ushered me down to the front row of discontentment.

See, rather than rejoicing in the birth announcement of my son, I allowed it to drive me into a deeper state of depression. I allowed it to push me into a selfish, depraved relationship with another woman. Wrapped up in the birth of my son was a whole paradigm of depression, selfishness, sinfulness, and depravity. The birth of my son was filled with resentment, frustration, and confusion. I resented my son. Oh how I hate to write that.

During the first few months of his life, I barely held him. I didn't want to. Statler and Waldorf were having their way with me. Oh, what I missed—until the divine appointment arrived.

Fast forward eight years to Bethel Church. That February day initiated a Holy Spirit experience that seated me in a new life with a new purpose. Although years earlier I had stopped seeing my son as a resentment, I had never viewed him as a redemption. That February at Bethel, I began to see him as redemption.

Today, my son and I have the greatest relationship. During the day, I look forward to our daily wrestling matches, or stepping on his Legos. I simply adore him; he has become a symbol of God's grace and redemption. And sometimes when I look into Judah's eyes, I swear I see the divine promise.

So when I heard the sentence, "God wants you to know that the situation in which your son was born into has been completely redeemed," I wept like a baby right there in the front row fifteen minutes before the music started.

After some reflection, I realized that it was February of 2011 when I decided to place the stake in the ground, leave the despair and depression of an affair, and begin the process of being redeemed. And now, seven years later to the month, complete redemption was ushered into my life.

Why seven years? In Hebrew, the number seven represents creation and perfection. The first sentence of the Bible is seven Hebrew words: In the beginning, God created the heavens and the earth. Out of the darkness, God spoke. His life-giving words ushered in a perfect universe that testifies to his glory. Out of darkness, his words created light and life. The old had become new, and the dead had come alive. There is always a newness, a creative redemption, with the breath of God. You and I are no different. His breath brings us to life.

Why seven years? Perhaps I could say it like this: a man in darkness redeemed by the breath of life as a new creation. I was reminded of the Exodus where the people of God were pinned down between the Red Sea and the approaching Pharaoh's army. Their options were limited: either try and swim for it and drown or be slaughtered by the army. With either option, death was inevitable.

Yet with God, there is always another option. Moses struck the sea with his staff, and the water was divided to allow safe passage for God's people as they fled from Pharaoh's army. The walls of water became a creation into a new life. As they passed through, with every step, they welcomed the arrival of freedom. Thoughts of pain, misery, and death melted away with every muddy step. Deliverance, grace, and freedom rose on the wings of hope with a new song.

There is a sea in front of you, stopping you from becoming what God has intended you to become. Maybe your sea is past sins that haunt you, or the lack of divine identity, or believing the jeers and heckles of Waldorf and Statler, or maybe it's the absence of the Perfect One who gives grace, celebration, and joy. Whatever it is, there is another way. Friends, your sea has been divided; the doorway has been created.

The question is, do you recognize the walls of water that were separated for your liberation? Just. Walk. Through. May you go and soak in the abundance of grace, waft in the fragrance of celebration, and dance in the joy of the Lord. May you find rest in being loved by Papa God exactly as you are. And may the jeers and heckles melt away at the presence of Holy Spirit as he comes and rests on you.

The Afterword to the Afterword

Although I find myself in redemption and hope under the shadow of Jesus, life is still full of wonder and mystery. Although my marriage has been redeemed, there are still areas that we wrestle with.

Victory is not perfection in everything, nor is it a destination. That's not what victory is in marriage. That may work for sports, but not marriages. Victory is the journey. It's one amazing—and sometimes agonizing—step after another not until you reach your destination, but rather stepping with arms around each other and hearts beating together. Victory in marriage is stepping as one in the same direction with the same purpose even through the despair and pain.

Although redeemed, our marriage is still difficult at times. Memories and dreams, for both of us, still sometimes haunt our lives. But now, we face them together, oftentimes through tears. And we have found that they are becoming less and less as time marches on.

Someone asked me the other day when I will be a pastor again. I shrugged; I don't know. Maybe that ship has sailed; maybe it is still docked waiting for me to climb aboard. I just have this feeling that the best is yet to come. And the voice of Holy Spirit has given me grace, celebration, and joy in the midst of unanswered questions and an uncertain future.

Take courage. Life for you may never be what it was. There may be new mountains and infinite oceans yet to explore. With a fresh breath from Holy Spirit, that exploration is fueled by a new grace, celebration, and joy in your life. And that, my friends, is a new creation.

Loved ones, grace is yours for the taking. Jesus offers it abundantly and freely. Within every difficulty and impossibility in your life, there is more than enough grace to sustain you. Your success depends on your receiving grace and then, in turn, offering grace to this world.

Beloved, your celebration awaits. No matter what circumstances you have experienced or are currently enduring, the presence of Jesus is standing like a rock. And he has offered you all that you need to make it through. Celebrate now with the coming victory.

Brothers and sisters, dance has a name, and it's joy. Take the time to make a joyful song, no matter the pitch. Take an evening and turn on some 80s music nice and loud and dance it out with your kids in the living room. You may be in pain, but joy will come in the morning.

Twenty years from now, you will regret more of what you didn't do than the mistakes you made. Extend your heart to the grace, celebration, and joy of Jesus. Breathe in the aroma of a life made just for you, yet long for ways to express your grace, celebration, and joy to the world around you. And choose which voice you will listen to.

The voices of Waldorf and Statler hold no power over you; those heckles from the balcony fall on your redeemed ears. Lift your heart; your redemption is here.

Notes

Introduction
1. See the truth of Psalm 139.
2. Genesis 28:16
3. Lawrence Kushner, *God Was in This Place And I, I Did Not Know* (Jewish Lights Publishing, 2002). This book is a great example of the Jewish search for biblical truth. There are seven chapters, with each chapter explaining a different interpretation of this one verse. Excellent book to read to see how a brilliant Jewish mind works.

Grace
4. "So now faith, hope, and love abide, these three; but the greatest of these is love" (1 Corinthians 13:13). Rabbis believe that the reason why love is the greatest is because in eternal life, hope will be nonexistent. What could you possibly hope for when confronted with utter perfection? And faith will diminish in the presence of God when our faith is made complete. Love, however, will be ever growing and expanding. Hence, love is the greatest.
5. Read anything by Dr. Skip Moen, a remarkable teacher on ancient Hebraic meanings.
6. TLC, "No Scrubs," 1999.
7. Ephesians 2:8
8. Lamentations 3:23
9. Mark 4:23
10. James 1:22
11. Genesis 1:4, 10, 12, 18, 21, 25, 31
12. Genesis 6:6
13. Romans 8:15
14. Galatians 4:7
15. John 1:1–2
16. "In the beginning, God created the heavens and the earth" (Genesis 1:1).
17. John 1:3
18. Matthew 6:10
19. *Tselem* is used fourteen times in the Old Testament, all of which contain negative implications, except the four uses in Genesis. This comparison suggests the

concept that after the fall of man, the use of *tselem* lost its divine value. It no longer referred to the likeness of God, but rather to creating graven images to be worshipped. The original *imago Dei* quickly diminished.

20. A big shout out to Quint Bryan, one of the greatest disciplers of his generation.
21. James 1:23–25
22. *Geneseos* was often translated as "genealogy" or "natural." It comes from the root word for *genesis*, meaning birth or beginning.
23. Exodus 3:7–8
24. Rob Bell and Don Golden, *Jesus Wants to Save Christians*.
25. A shout out to Pastor Dan Cale. This phrase came from PD during one of our many, many conversations. Holy Spirit used him to mend deep wounds. I am forever grateful for his friendship and leadership. Much respect and love goes to the master hunter from PA. PS: After further dialogue, I learned it came from Star Trek.
26. Luke 15:11–20

Celebration

27. Exodus 1:8–14
28. Exodus 2
29. "This day shall be for you a memorial day, and you shall keep it as a feast to the Lord; throughout your generations, as a statute forever, you shall keep it as a feast" (Exodus 12:14).
30. Luke 2:4
31. Luke 2:7a
32. Luke 2:7b
33. Matthew 2:8
34. Alfred Edersheim, *The Life and Times of Jesus the Messiah, Volume 1* (Hindrickson Publishers: 1993), 131.
35. Rob Bell, *Drop Like Stars*
36. Exodus 8–12
37. Exodus 12
38. Exodus 8–12. As the ten plagues were initiated, livestock died and ultimately all the first born of Egypt died. The Jewish people do not celebrate death, but rather celebrate with the understanding that their freedom came at an immense cost to life.
39. First Kings 19:1
40. First Kings 19:4
41. I heard Ran Vander Laan say this to a group he was teaching.
42. I heard Ran Vander Laan say this to a group he was teaching.
43. Psalm 23:1–2
44. First Kings 19:5–6
45. Exodus 4:18
46. John 20:19–20

47. I'm pretty sure this is from Bill Johnson, Bethel Church in Redding, California. I couldn't find it in his books, but it sure sounds like him.
48. John 19:25–27
49. John 18:22
50. See Nick Page, *The Longest Week* (Hodder & Stoughton, 2009).
51. Exodus 24:12–15

Joy

52. James 1:4
53. Second Corinthians 12:9
54. Second Samuel 6:16
55. Joel 2:5
56. Again, read Dr. Skip Moen.
57. Paul calls Jesus the wisdom of God in 1 Corinthians 1:24. In addition, I believe Wisdom in Proverbs 8 is the personification of a divine trait through which the Son manifests himself. Thirdly, the *logos* in John 1 carries connotations of "wisdom" throughout first-century Greek literature. See
58. "Call to me and I will answer you, and will tell you great and hidden things that you have not known" (Jeremiah 33:3).
59. Mark 16:3
60. Matthew 27:66
61. Matthew 28:2
62. Ephesians 1:20–21
63. Isaiah 32:1–2
64. "Then Jacob went on his journey and came to the land of the people of the east. As he looked, he saw a well in the field, and behold, three flocks of sheep lying beside it, for out of that well the flocks were watered. The stone on the well's mouth was large, and when all the flocks were gathered there, the shepherds would roll the stone from the mouth of the well and water the sheep, and put the stone back in its place over the mouth of the well. Jacob said to them, 'My brothers, where do you come from?'

    "They said, 'We are from Haran.'

    "He said to them, 'Do you know Laban the son of Nahor?'

    "They said, 'We know him.'

    "He said to them, 'Is it well with him?'

    "They said, 'It is well; and see, Rachel his daughter is coming with the sheep!'

    "He said, 'Behold, it is still high day; it is not time for the livestock to be gathered together. Water the sheep and go, pasture them.'

    "But they said, 'We cannot until all the flocks are gathered together and the stone is rolled from the mouth of the well; then we water the sheep'" (Genesis 29:1–8).
65. Check out Ecclesiastes 9:7; Isaiah 24:11; Revelation 6:6; Joel 3:18; Psalm 104:15; Amos 9:12–15; Isaiah 55:1; Judges 9:13

66. John 2
67. An ancient story of Plutarch states that when Anthony entered the city of Ephesus, "women arrayed like Bacchanals, and men and boys like Satyrs and Pans led the way before him and the city was full of ivy and thyruswands and harps and pipes and flutes, the people hailing him as Dionysus, giver of Joy and Beneficent." See Cleon L. Rogers Jr., "The Dionysian Background of Ephesians 5:18," *Bibliotheca Sacra* 136, no. 543 (July 1979): 249–257.
68. John B. Polhill, "John 1–4: The Revelation of True Life," *Review & Expositor* 85, no. 3 (1988): 445–457.
69. Colossians 3:15–17
70. Luke 24:32
71. Isaiah 42:9–10
72. You must read Brian McLaren, *A New Kind of Christianity* (HarperCollins, 2010).

About the Author

Jeremiah and Elisha Kutz are founders of All Things New, Christian Marriage Coaching focused on healing and redemption within marriages. They are passionate about joining Holy Spirit in creating prophetic atmospheres in every area of life.

He has been a missionary for two years and a pastor for ten. His passion is for equipping the church to live out their destiny as they usher in the kingdom of God. Jeremiah is absolutely in love with the church and desires to disciple this coming generation to renew their culture.

Jeremiah's love for knowledge has earned him three master's degrees in theology. His love for the original languages and culture of the Bible usher his audiences into a deep encounter with Jesus. His pursuit of the presence of Jesus has led him to discover his true identity as a child of God and coheir with Christ.

Jeremiah and Elisha have been married for eighteen years and have three powerful children.

Visit jeremiahkutz.com for additional resources.

CPSIA information can be obtained
at www.ICGtesting.com
Printed in the USA
FFHW021704150919
54992922-60703FF